"He opened His mouth and taught them…"

—Matthew 5:2

Your Faith Has Saved You

Homilies for Liturgical Year A
Sundays, Solemnities, and Some Feasts

Rev. John P. Cush, STD

En Route Books and Media, LLC
Saint Louis, MO

✪ENROUTE
Make the time

En Route Books and Media, LLC

5705 Rhodes Avenue

St. Louis, MO 63109

Contact us at

contactus@enroutebooksandmedia.com

Cover Credit: Sebastian Mahfood using
St. Matthew and the Angel (1661) by Rembrandt (1606-1669)
courtesy of Wikimedia Commons

Copyright 2025 John P. Cush

ISBN-13: 979-8-88870-487-5
Library of Congress Control Number:
Available online at https://catalog.loc.gov

Dedication

To the Most Reverend Paul R. Sanchez, S.T.L., D.D.,
who is an exemplary priest

Table of Contents

"You are the Christ"
The Christology of Saint Matthew's Gospel

At the heart of the Gospel according to Saint Matthew is a burning question—posed first by Jesus Himself, and still reverberating in every homily, every proclamation of the Word, and every heart that listens with faith: "But who do you say that I am?" (Mt 16:15)

Peter's response—"*You are the Christ, the Son of the living God*" (Mt 16:16)—forms the cornerstone of the Matthean Gospel and the foundation of apostolic preaching. Saint Matthew writes not simply to recount the life of Jesus, but to bear witness to His identity, to form disciples who recognize the Messiah in the crucified and risen Lord, and to commission the Church to proclaim that identity to the nations (Mt 28:19–20). His Gospel, then, is deeply Christological, presenting Jesus as the fulfillment of Israel's hopes, the true Son of God, and the eschatological Emmanuel—God with us(Mt 1:23; 28:20).

This introduction explores the shape of Matthew's Christology and its implications for preaching and hearing the Word today.

The opening verse of the Gospel provides a genealogy, but also a theological lens: "*The book of the genealogy of Jesus Christ, the son of David, the son of Abraham*" (Mt 1:1). For Matthew, Christ's identity is rooted in salvation history. Jesus is not a new teaching but the fulfillment of the Law and the Prophets (Mt 5:17). He is the promised Messiah—Davidic King and heir of the covenant with Abraham through whom all nations will be blessed (cf. Gen 12:3).

Matthew reveals a Jesus who recapitulates Israel's vocation: He relives the Exodus, ascends the mountain to give the New Law (Mt

5–7), and establishes a new twelve-fold Israel in the Apostles. Christ is thus the embodiment of Israel's story, not abolishing the old but fulfilling it in Himself.

For the preacher, this Christology reminds us that the Gospel must be proclaimed not as an abstraction or moral code, but as the culmination of God's covenantal fidelity—a story fulfilled in Christ and continuing in the Church.

From the announcement to Joseph to the final promise of the Risen Lord, Matthew's Gospel is framed by the mystery of Emmanuel—"God with us." This title, drawn from Isaiah 7:14 and confirmed in the child born of Mary (Mt 1:23), is not poetic metaphor. It is a theological declaration: in Jesus, God has come to dwell among His people, not simply in word or vision, but in the flesh.

Matthew's Christ is not merely a prophet or sage. He is the One who speaks with divine authority: *"You have heard it said… but I say to you"* (Mt 5:21–22); the One to whom even the winds and sea obey (Mt 8:27); the One whose word judges (Mt 7:24–27) and saves. His authority is not given—it is intrinsic.

This high Christology is confirmed in the post-resurrection commission: *"All authority in heaven and on earth has been given to me… and behold, I am with you always"* (Mt 28:18, 20). Christ is not only the content of preaching—He is its living and abiding presence. The homily, therefore, is never merely exposition; it is an encounter with Emmanuel, the One who still speaks in His Church.

Matthew's Gospel is often called the Gospel of the Kingdom, and rightly so (cf. Mt 4:17; 13). Yet the path to kingship in Matthew is paradoxical: the Messiah reigns through suffering, and the Kingdom is revealed in the Cross. The climactic passion narrative (Mt 26–27) shows the Son of Man, Daniel's glorious figure (Dan 7:13), willingly humiliated, mocked, and crucified. Glory is inseparable from obedience. Jesus is a king who reigns from the Cross because He is the Son who always does the will of the Father." The crucified Christ is not defeated; He is revealed. His kingship is hidden beneath rejection, but confirmed in the Resurrection, when He is declared with finality as "Son of God in power" (cf. Rom 1:4; Mt 28:6–10).

This paradox is not only theological but homiletic. The preacher must always announce the Paschal shape of the Gospel: that Christ's path is downward, into suffering and death, and only then upward into glory. The Sunday homily must lead the faithful not merely to admire Jesus but to follow Him in the obedience of faith, trusting that suffering with Him leads to resurrection.

As we have seen in the readings at the end of the liturgical year, Matthew's Christ is not only the historical Jesus but the Eschatological Judge. In the parables of Matthew 25, He comes at midnight, returns to settle accounts, and separates the nations according to love (Mt 25:1–46). The parables are not literary ornaments. They are Christ's own self-revelation as the One who will return to judge the living and the dead.

But the Judge is also the Bridegroom—the One who desires to draw the soul into union. The Christ of Matthew is not only just—He is burning with longing for the return of His people. His judgment reveals not legalism, but whether the soul has welcomed His mercy and responded in kind.

This eschatological Christology demands that preaching, especially on Sundays and solemnities, form the faithful in vigilance. Not in anxiety, but in hope. Every Mass is a preparation for the Lord's return. Every homily is a call to be found faithful—*"Blessed is that servant whom the Master finds at work when He returns"* (Mt 24:46).

In the Gospel of Matthew, the preacher is given no generic figure, but Jesus the Christ—Son of David, Son of God, Son of Man. He fulfills the Scriptures, embodies God's presence, suffers and reigns, and will come again in glory. The Gospel is not simply about Jesus. It is Jesus Himself, given and proclaimed.

The task of the homilist, then, is not first to moralize or entertain, but to open the Scriptures and reveal Christ, as He opened His mouth and taught them (Mt 5:2). The preacher, like the wise scribe trained for the Kingdom (Mt 13:52), must bring forth treasures both old and new—faithful to the tradition, alive in the Spirit, and aflame with the desire to say, with Peter and the Church: *"You are the Christ."*

John P. Cush, STD
Saint Joseph's Seminary and College, Yonkers, New York
October 20, 2025

Eight Theological Themes in the Gospel of Saint Matthew for Preaching (Year A)

1. Fulfillment of the Scriptures

"All this took place to fulfill what the Lord had spoken by the prophet" (Mt 1:22).

Matthew's Gospel is deeply rooted in a theology of fulfillment (*pleroma*), portraying Jesus as the telos of the Law and the Prophets. His frequent use of formula quotations (cf. Mt 2:5, 2:15, 2:17, 2:23, etc.) signals a Christocentric hermeneutic grounded in typology. Saint Jerome notes, "The entire series of the Old Testament prophecies converge on the coming of Christ" (*Commentary on Matthew*).

The *Catena Aurea* records Rabanus Maurus commenting on Matthew 1:22: "The Evangelist proves that the conception was wonderful by the authority of a prophet." Thus, homilists must help the faithful see Christ as the culmination of the divine economy, "the center and fullness of the entire economy of salvation" (CCC 112).

Each Sunday Gospel becomes an opportunity to illuminate the continuity of the two Testaments, with Jesus as the interpretive key. Christ is not only the fulfillment but the exegete of Scripture (cf. Lk 24:27).

2. Jesus as the New Moses and Giver of the New Law

"Seeing the crowds, he went up on the mountain... and he opened his mouth and taught them" (Mt 5:1-2).

Matthew presents Jesus as the New Moses, the authoritative interpreter of the Law who delivers the definitive Torah from the mount. Five great discourses structure the Gospel (chs. 5-7, 10, 13, 18, 24-25), mirroring the five books of the Pentateuch.

In the *Catena Aurea*, Saint Augustine sees the Sermon on the Mount as the fulfillment of the Law through grace: "He teaches the Law, not to destroy it, but to fulfill it."

Aquinas writes that Christ, as true God and true Lawgiver, perfects the Old Law by interiorizing it: "The New Law is chiefly the grace of the Holy Ghost, which is given to those who believe in Christ" (*STh* I-II, q.106, a.1).

The preacher must reveal not merely the moral demands of Christ's teaching, but the grace that makes them possible. The Beatitudes are not ideals but revelations of the form of sanctity in Christ.

3. The Kingdom of Heaven: Already and Not Yet

"Repent, for the kingdom of heaven is at hand" (Mt 4:17).

Matthew uniquely prefers "Kingdom of Heaven" over "Kingdom of God" (used in Mark and Luke), emphasizing its eschatological origin and divine character. The Kingdom arrives in Jesus, grows in the Church, and will be consummated at the end of time.

Saint John Chrysostom comments: "He does not say that the kingdom shall be at hand, but that it is at hand; for that which shall be hereafter is not the kingdom, but the judgment" (*Hom. in Matt.* 14).

The Catechism teaches that "The Kingdom of God has come in the person of Christ" and is made present in the Church (CCC 763-764), though "its full consummation will not come until the Lord returns" (CCC 1042).

The homily must proclaim the Kingdom as both present in grace and future in glory. Encourage the faithful to live now as citizens of that Kingdom—by works of mercy, fidelity, and prayer.

4. Jesus as Emmanuel: God With Us

"They shall name him Emmanuel, which means, God with us" (Mt 1:23).

Matthew's Gospel is bracketed by this promise of divine presence: at the beginning (1:23) and end (28:20: *"I am with you always"*). Jesus is Emmanuel in His Incarnation and continues as Emmanuel in the sacraments, the Church, and the poor (cf. Mt 25:40).

The *Catena Aurea* cites Saint Remigius: "He is called 'God with us' to show that His divinity is inseparable from His humanity."

The Catechism states, "Jesus Christ is true God and true man, in the unity of His divine person" (CCC 464). His presence "remains ever active in the Church" (CCC 1088).

In preaching, underscore that God is not distant. The Eucharist is the continuing Emmanuel. The homily itself becomes a sacramental means of Christ's presence and voice (cf. *Verbum Domini* 59).

5. Christ the Judge and Bridegroom

"Behold, the bridegroom! Come out to meet him!" (Mt 25:6); *"He will separate them one from another..."* (Mt 25:32).

Matthew's eschatology climaxes in the parables of chapters 24–25, where Jesus appears as both the Bridegroom (Mt 25:1–13) and the Judge (Mt 25:31–46). These roles are not contradictory but complementary.

Saint Gregory the Great wrote: "The Judge comes, and He is also the Bridegroom. Let us prepare our lamps that we may go forth to meet Him" (*Hom. in Evang.* 12).

Aquinas explains that the final judgment reveals whether one has been united to Christ through grace: "To be judged is to be measured by the form of Christ" (*STh* III, q.59, a.1).

The preacher must awaken the faithful to spiritual vigilance and nuptial hope. The Lord comes not only to judge but to espouse the soul to Himself forever (cf. Hos 2:16-20).

6. Discipleship and the Narrow Path

"Enter through the narrow gate..." (Mt 7:13); *"Take my yoke upon you and learn from me..."* (Mt 11:29).

Discipleship in Matthew requires moral transformation, radical trust, and continual conversion. Christ's invitation is universal, but the way is narrow and requires grace-fueled perseverance.

In the *Catena Aurea*, Saint Hilary writes: "The gate is narrow, because it is difficult to believe, and because few are they that do believe."

The Catechism teaches: "Discipleship entails accepting the Cross of Christ, mortifying the passions, and walking in newness of life" (CCC 2015).

The homily must not soften the demands of discipleship but frame them within divine grace and eschatological reward: the Cross is the narrow gate, but it opens onto the Kingdom.

7. The Church and the Apostolic Mission

"You are Peter, and upon this rock I will build my Church" (Mt 16:18); *"Go, therefore, and make disciples of all nations..."* (Mt 28:19).

Only Matthew uses the word "Church" (ekklesia). Christ founds His Church on Peter, giving him the keys (Mt 16:19), and sends the Apostles with universal authority at the Gospel's end.

Saint Cyprian declares: "He who has not the Church for his mother cannot have God for his Father" (*De Unit. Eccles.* 6).

The Catechism affirms that the Church is "the seed and beginning of the Kingdom" (CCC 763) and "the universal sacrament of salvation" (CCC 774).

As homilists, we must emphasize the visibility and apostolicity of the Church. Foster love for the Church as Christ's Bride and instrument, and encourage active fidelity to her teaching and mission.

8. Mercy and Forgiveness: The Heart of the Father

"Forgive us our debts, as we also have forgiven our debtors" (Mt 6:12); *"Should you not have had mercy...?"*(Mt 18:33).

Matthew offers some of the most powerful teachings on forgiveness in the New Testament: the Lord's Prayer (Mt 6), the parable of the unforgiving servant (Mt 18), and Jesus' command to forgive seventy times seven (Mt 18:22).

Saint John Chrysostom observes: "Nothing makes us so like God as our readiness to forgive."

The Catechism teaches that "forgiveness is the fundamental condition of the reconciliation of the children of God with their Father" (CCC 2844). This mercy is most perfectly mediated in the Sacrament of Penance (CCC 1468).

As homilists, we must center the homily on divine mercy, especially in Lent and Ordinary Time. Encourage frequent Confession and the imitation of the Father's mercy in family and society.

Together, these eight themes form a coherent theological and pastoral framework for preaching from Saint Matthew's Gospel. They flow organically from the inspired text, receive authoritative interpretation in the Tradition, and point the faithful toward deeper communion with Jesus Christ—"Son of David, Son of Abraham," the New Moses, Emmanuel, Bridegroom, and Judge, who is present now in His Church and will come again in glory.

First Sunday of Advent

Today marks the beginning of the Year of Grace 2023. Yes, even though the calendar year is not yet over, and for us who are teachers, the academic year certainly isn't over, the Church's liturgical year, which we call "The Year of Grace" is over as of yesterday's Saturday morning Mass. We are in a brand-new year.

And, as we know, the Church's year begins with Advent, this four-week preparation time for Christmas. So, let's look into what makes Advent so important:

It is a four-week period of preparation. Advent is a season of longing, which is why the color of Advent in the liturgy is violet, a color which indicates prayerful penitential preparation. In fact, it's preparation for three important aspects of our faith.

First, we commemorate the fact that, at the end of time, when Christ is all in all, he will come again in glory to judge the living and the dead, and, of his Kingdom, there will be no end. Yes, Advent reminds us of the four last things, eschatology, namely death, judgment, Heaven, and hell. Christ will again to judge us, in our own particular judgement at the moment of our death, and, in the fullness of time, Christ will come to give judgement to the Universe, to every living soul, and Christ the King of the Universe, whom we celebrated liturgically last week, will come to create a new Heaven and a new Earth.

The whole first part of Advent is all about this aspect, up until December 17, when we switch our perspective to the second aspect of Advent. The key figures for us to focus upon during this first part of Advent is the Prophet Isaiah from the Old Testament and from the

New Testament, the last and the greatest of the Prophets, Saint John the Baptist. We might call this time period "remote preparation for Christmas."

Second, we commemorate the fact that, in the fullness of time, the Eternal Word of God, the Second Person of the Most Blessed Trinity, was incarnate (meaning, became man) in the womb of the perpetually Virgin Mary and was born. We celebrate the fact that, at a certain time, in a certain place, our Lord Jesus, God, entered into history, to save us from our sins. So, we celebrate the coming of Christ into history over 2,000 years ago. The reason why we use candles on the Advent wreath, which the longer we burn them get smaller, is to indicate Christ's entrance into history. Note that the wreath, like time, is circular and is green, indicating the new life that only Christ can bring. The first two candles of the wreath are violet, the third rose (which is a mixture of the violet of Advent and the joyful white of Christmas) to signify joy, and the fourth candle is violet.

This whole second part of Advent is like a "proximate preparation" for Christmas and the figure who dominates this section is, of course, Our Lady of the New Advent, the Blessed Virgin Mary.

Third, and finally, we commemorate that Christ needs to be born again, each day, he needs to come each day into our hearts, our minds, and our souls. We need to put on the mind of Christ, to see with the eyes of Christ, to love with the heart of Christ, and to work to help our sisters and brothers in the world today with the hands of Christ. Advent reminds us that we are called to see, to recognize, no, rather, to perceive Christ in every single soul we encounter, for each and every human being is created in God's own image and likeness and each and every soul has immortal dignity which needs to be preserved and celebrated.

So, what spiritual practices can we do in order to prepare in his Holy season of Advent? May I please suggest three?

First, read from the Gospel of Matthew, chapters 1 and 2, as well as the Gospel of Luke, chapters 1 to 4, a little bit each day and reflect on the Gospel passages and how it relates to you in your own life and in your own particular circumstances. We have four weeks. Perhaps we could read only a few sentences a day in our Bibles.

Second, pray daily the Holy Rosary. When we pray the Holy Rosary, we reflect on the mysteries of the life of Our Lord and Our Lady and, in this reflection, we can grow closer to the reality of what occurred in the life of Christ and the life of Our Lady.

Third, and finally, perhaps we might wish to avail ourselves of the sacrament of Penance. Going to confession in Advent is a great practice to prepare ourselves for the eschatological (those four last things which you heard me mention at the start of this homily) and also to help us allow Christ to be born in our heart each day.

Second Sunday of Advent

As we celebrate this Second Sunday of Advent, the violet vestments, the unlit candles still awaiting their flame, and the stark voice of John the Baptist remind us that Advent is not yet Christmas. It is a time of hopeful preparation and interior purification. The Church, like a wise mother, calls us not to rush toward the joy of Christ's birth but to make room for Him by repentance, prayer, and patient expectation.

The first reading from Isaiah gives us the breathtaking image of the *shoot that shall sprout from the stump of Jesse* (Isa 11:1). Here, the prophet speaks of the coming Messiah, one anointed with the Spirit of the Lord — of wisdom, understanding, counsel, and fear of the Lord. The Fathers of the Church saw in this passage a direct prophecy of Jesus Christ. Saint Jerome writes that "the rod is the holy Virgin Mary, and the flower that comes forth from her is Christ." This is not merely poetic — it speaks of the Incarnation as a work both hidden and miraculous, God springing new life from what seemed cut down.

Saint Thomas Aquinas, in his *Catena Aurea*, reflects on the gifts of the Spirit listed by Isaiah and teaches that these gifts perfect the theological virtues in us. For instance, the gift of wisdom perfects charity, the gift of understanding perfects faith. Thus, Isaiah is not only describing the Messiah but also outlining what Christ wishes to bestow upon His Church. Aquinas reminds us that Christ's anointing is not just for Himself but is shared with His mystical body — you and me — through grace. This is the goal of Advent: to receive the Spirit more deeply and to let it transform our lives.

Saint Paul, in the second reading from Romans, exhorts us to endurance, encouragement, and unity, saying that "whatever was written previously was written for our instruction, that by endurance and by the encouragement of the Scriptures we might have hope" (Rom 15:4). This is particularly apt in Advent, a season of longing and hope. Saint John Chrysostom notes that Paul places endurance first because "tribulation and toil precede consolation and joy." Our waiting is not passive but full of yearning and the sanctifying fire of patience.

Then comes the voice crying in the wilderness: *"Repent, for the kingdom of heaven is at hand!"* (Matt 3:2). John the Baptist appears in the desert like Elijah of old, clothed in camel's hair, eating locusts and wild honey — a sign of austerity and urgency. The Church Fathers saw John as the "last of the prophets and the first of the apostles," the bridge between Old and New. Origen wrote that John "was the friend of the Bridegroom who prepares the Bride for Him by repentance."

Yet John does not merely ask for private remorse; he demands *fruit worthy of repentance*. Advent is not a season for vague spiritual sentiment but for concrete change. Do we treat others with justice? Do we live in peace, as Isaiah prophesied — where the wolf and the lamb dwell together? Do we welcome others as Christ welcomed us, as Paul says? The fire that John speaks of is either purifying or consuming. Saint Augustine warns us, "If you fear the coming of the Lord, then change your life. He will come, whether you wish it or not."

But John's fiery message is not meant to bring despair. The axe at the root is a call to awaken. The winnowing fan is the breath of the

Spirit separating sin from grace. The coming of the Lord is both judgment and salvation. And so Advent teaches us to prepare not only to commemorate Christ's first coming in Bethlehem but to be ready for His glorious return.

Dear friends, in this second week of Advent, let us heed the call of John. Let us go to confession, open the Scriptures, fast a little, and prepare a space in our hearts where the flower from Jesse's root may bloom. As Saint Bernard of Clairvaux taught, Christ comes in three ways: in history at Bethlehem, in mystery through grace, and in majesty at the end of time. May our Advent longing embrace all three, and may we be found ready — not only with candles lit, but with hearts enkindled

Third Sunday of Advent

In the Gospel we proclaim this Sunday from the Evangelist Matthew, we encounter, yet again, the figure of Saint John the Baptist. At this time in the Gospel story, John is already imprisoned, locked away by Herod. The Lord Jesus had John's disciples come to him, asking quite bluntly if he's the one about whom John was preaching, the long awaited Messiah of Israel.

Although only Luke's Gospel actually comes out and states that John was the blood relative, the cousin of the Lord Jesus, we know for certain that there was a strong, intrinsic bond between John the Baptist and Jesus. Jesus Himself proclaims the fact that there is no man born of woman greater than John the Baptist. In fact, there were many, many people who truly believed that John was the Christ and there were many, many people who left everything to go and follow him. One of the reasons why the story of the baptism of the Lord by John in the Jordan is featured in all four of the Gospels is to serve as a reminder to all that it is Jesus, not John, who is the Holy One of God, the Messiah. John, in all four accounts from the Gospel, is the first to recognize the adult Jesus as Lord, and, in fact, protests vehemently the mere suggestion that he should baptize Jesus.

There must have been a reason why so many people believed that John was the Messiah at first. For starters, he fit the part of the Old Testament prophet much more than did Jesus. John, with his clothes of camel hair and the leather belt around his waist, looked the part. With his diet of wild honey and locust, and, above all, his consistent message of repentance in preparation for the coming of the Kingdom of God, John, perhaps even more so than Jesus, looked like a new version of Hosea, with his outrageous stunts to make his point, or a new Ezekiel, a new Isaiah or, perhaps even more, a new Elijah.

Imagine being John the Baptist. Imagine the whole world hanging on your every word, your every action. Imagine the feeling of power, the feeling of euphoria. They all want you; they all need you. Now, remember that messiahs, or rather people claiming to be the messiah, were a dime a dozen in Jerusalem. Every single Jewish mother was hoping and praying that it would be her little boy who would grow up to be the savior of his people. And, I'd venture to guess, perhaps Elizabeth was the same.

And yet, John does not let the fame, the adulation go to his head. He knows who he is and what it is that he is meant to be. "Not me, but thee, O Lord." "He must increase, I must decrease." Or, as he states in another Gospel passage, "One mightier than I is coming after me. I am not worthy to stoop and loosen the thongs of his sandals. I have baptized you with water; he will baptize you with the Holy Spirit."

John is able to do this because he knows who he is: he is not the messiah, but the forerunner of the Messiah, the last and greatest of the Prophets, the one selected from all eternity to point the way to the Lamb of God, who is going to take away the sins of the world. John knows that he is a beloved child of God Most High, one created in the image and likeness of Almighty God, and one who will be bathed in the most precious blood of the Lamb who will be slain for us men and our salvation. And that's enough for him. This is true humility, true openness to the will of the Lord in our life. This can only come from self-knowledge and confidence in the place that the Lord has for us in the building up of his Kingdom.

How about for us? Do we know, really know, who we are? Do we recognize that we are not the Messiah? That God is God and that we're not God, and thank God for that? Do we recognize that we are creature, not creator, completely totally dependent on the one who loves us, that every breath we take is totally dependent on the gracious will of our Heavenly Father?

The Ancient Greek aphorism "know thyself", is one of the Delphic maxims and was inscribed in the *pronaos* of the Temple of Apollo at Delphi according to the Greek periegetic writer Pausanias. Do you and I know ourselves, really know ourselves? Do I trust that, for some reason known only to God, in spite of my sinful ways and my human limitations, I was chosen to be his priest, and so too are all my brother priests? Do you in consecrated life recognize that, for no other reason besides the will of the Heavenly Father, you were chosen to be a Bride of Christ, with your vows of poverty, chastity, and obedience, all true eschatological signs of the Kingdom of God which John was born to preach and which Jesus is in his very Divine Person? Do you in your own particular vocation in this Christian life, married, single, recognize who you are, how beautiful your are, another beloved daughter or son of God the Most High?

The 20th century spiritual writer Thomas Merton, after many years of living the Trappist lifestyle, was permitted to leave his abbey to go shopping for his community one day. This is from his work, *Conjectures of a Guilty Bystander*:

"In Louisville, at the corner of Fourth and Walnut, in the center of the shopping district, I was suddenly overwhelmed with the realization that I loved all those people, that they were mine

and I theirs, that we could not be alien to one another even though we were total strangers. It was like waking from a dream of separateness, of spurious self-isolation in a special world, the world of renunciation and supposed holiness... This sense of liberation from an illusory difference was such a relief and such a joy to me that I almost laughed out loud... I have the immense joy of being man, a member of a race in which God Himself became incarnate. As if the sorrows and stupidities of the human condition could overwhelm me, now I realize what we all are. And if only everybody could realize this! But it cannot be explained. There is no way of telling people that they are all walking around shining like the sun."

You're all walking around, shining like the sun. Despite sorrow, despite sin, you and I are created in God's image and through baptism are conformed to his likeness. On your worst day, when everything seems to be going wrong, don't lose sight of that.

Fourth Sunday of Advent

The Gospel we proclaim today, taken from the Evangelist Matthew, puts the focus firmly on Saint Joseph, the husband of Mary. Joseph stands as a model of what every single Catholic man (or woman, for that matter!) should be. Joseph was truly obedient to the will of God in his life. The angel tells Joseph to "(H)ave no fear about taking Mary to be your wife." As soon as Joseph knew God's will for him, he obeyed. When the angel told Joseph that Herod was planning to destroy the child, Joseph immediately got up and began the flight to Egypt. He didn't negotiate the plans; he wasn't texting Mary to see what she thought about it. He knew what he had to do for his wife and his son, the Son of God really, and he did it. Imagine the impact of going into Egypt. We know what Egypt meant to the Jewish people historically. It would be like a modern day Jew running to modern day Auschwitz to search for safety. And yet, he accepts. As Moses led his people out of Egypt, this Joseph follows the example of that other "master dreamer," Joseph of the Book of Genesis and establishes a place in Egypt for his people, his humble wife and unborn child.

Often, when we think of Joseph, we only think about his relationship with our Lord. I'd like to put the focus on the relationship with his wife. Much of our tradition posits Joseph as old. This is due to the apocryphal writings of the early church, ancient writings which were not divinely inspired, or approved by the Church as canonical. Some of these ancient writings say that when Joseph married the Blessed Mother he was 89 years old, and that he died at the age of 111. That's pretty amazing. There is really nothing in the Bible to suggest that St. Joseph was so old. We can be assured that Mary didn't have to push St. Joseph in a wheel chair through Nazareth. Even in the ancient catacomb of Priscilla, Joseph was drawn without a beard showing him to be a younger man. He was obviously older than the Blessed Mother; perhaps in his thirties, while she was much younger. Joseph was Mary's guardian and protector.

A younger man, with his whole life, in front of him; well, at least as long as the average life span of a man was back then. His whole concept of his relationship with his wife had to change. What he thought would have been their relationship, what he thought would have been the family that they would have raised together, well, that all had to change.

I think that for Joseph, the just man, he must truly have loved, really intensely loved Mary. What he does for her is not just out of duty and piety. He does what he does because he truly, deeply, chastely loves her and was totally devoted to her, going far above and beyond. Joseph loved his wife and he would do anything for her, even giving up everything he has and knows for her. That flight into Egypt is something that I keep thinking about lately. He adores his wife; he trusts her. And when her son, the Son of God, is born, he loves her even more because of Jesus.

Joseph was an obedient man. Whenever he was warned in a dream, he always obeyed the will of God. Even though Mary was far along in her pregnancy, Joseph had to believe it was God's will for them to leave Nazareth and go down to Bethlehem to fulfill the prophecy of Micah that the Savior would be born in Bethlehem. Joseph abandoned himself to the will of God. I wonder if I could have that trust. He knows that it won't be easy, not for him, not for his wife, and not for their son, Jesus. But he trusts.

Can I do that? Can I trust in my own vocation? Can you? Can you and I trust that the Lord has placed everything in our midst, everyone in our lives, for a reason, and be open, attentive, reasonable, loving, honest, before the face of God, before the will of God in our lives? This is the challenge, this is the example of Joseph, the one who adores Mary and Jesus, for each of us in our lives.

The Immaculate Conception

Today the Church rejoices in one of the most sublime mysteries of our faith — the Immaculate Conception of the Blessed Virgin Mary, the truth that, from the first moment of her conception, Mary was preserved immune from all stain of original sin by the singular grace and privilege of Almighty God and in view of the merits of Jesus Christ, the Savior of the human race. This dogma, solemnly defined by Pope Pius IX in *Ineffabilis Deus* (1854), affirms:

"The most Blessed Virgin Mary was, from the first moment of her conception, by a singular grace and privilege of Almighty God and in view of the merits of Jesus Christ... preserved free from all stain of original sin" (*DS* 2803).

This is not merely a devotional flourish, but a truth at the heart of the mystery of salvation. For how fitting it is that she who would bear the All-Holy Son of God should herself be wholly holy — a *sanctuary unviolated*, a *living Ark of the Covenant*.

In the first reading from Genesis, we hear the aftermath of the Fall. But even as God pronounces judgment, He sows the seed of hope in what the Church has long called the *Protoevangelium* — the "first Gospel":

"I will put enmity between you and the woman, and between your offspring and hers" (Gen 3:15).

The Church Fathers saw in this mysterious woman not merely Eve but Mary, the New Eve. As Saint Irenaeus declared:

"And thus also it was that the knot of Eve's disobedience was loosed by the obedience of Mary. For what the virgin Eve had bound fast through unbelief, this did the Virgin Mary set free through faith.

For just as the former was led astray by the word of an angel so that she fled from God, so the latter received the good tidings by means of the word of an angel so that she bore God within her." (*Adversus Haereses* V.19.1)

In Mary, we see the full reversal of the Fall. Eve's disobedience opened the door to sin; Mary's obedient *fiat* opened the door to salvation. Thus, the enmity God placed between the serpent and "the woman" is fulfilled most perfectly in her absolute sinlessness.

Many Fathers of the Church, while not yet formulating the dogma as we know it today, gave powerful witness to Mary's all-holiness. Saint Ephrem the Syrian sang:

"You and your mother are alone in this: You are wholly beautiful, and in you there is no blemish."

And again:

"As lightning is not sullied by contact with mud, so the Mother of God was not defiled by sin."

Saint Ambrose of Milan wrote:

"Mary, a virgin not only undefiled but a virgin whom grace has made inviolate, free of every stain of sin."

These patristic reflections echo the angel Gabriel's greeting in today's Gospel:

"*Hail, full of grace, the Lord is with you*" (Luke 1:28).

The Greek *kecharitōmenē* is not merely a polite greeting. It is a title — *she who has been and remains filled with grace*. As Blessed John Duns Scotus taught, this fullness of grace must logically include preservation from original sin: "*Potuit, decuit, ergo fecit*" — *God could do it; it was fitting that He do it; therefore, He did it.*

Scotus argued that preservative redemption is even more perfect than restorative redemption. Why should Christ be less powerful in His mother than in others? In Mary, He exercised His redemptive power preemptively, keeping her from falling into the pit rather than lifting her out of it.

Saint Paul, in our second reading from Ephesians, tells us that God "chose us in Christ before the foundation of the world, to be holy and blameless before Him" (Eph 1:4). If this applies to all the baptized, how much more to her who bore Christ in her very flesh?

Mary is the first fruit of the redeemed, chosen not merely for her own sake but for ours. Her sinlessness is not a barrier between us and her — it is the very guarantee that she is the *perfect intercessor*, a mother with a heart utterly conformed to God's will.

In this holy season of Advent, as we await the coming of Christ, Mary appears not only as the one who awaited Him most perfectly, but as the model of the Church, the *ecclesia immaculata*. As Pope Pius IX wrote: "She appeared in the world radiant with that innocence, that original justice, and that holiness which Adam lost for himself and for all his descendants in his unhappy fall."

Let us then look to Mary, not with distant admiration, but with hopeful imitation. She is the mirror in which we see the destiny God intends for all His children — to be *holy and without blemish before Him in love*.

Let us entrust ourselves to her maternal intercession. Let us ask her, the Immaculate Conception, to form Christ anew in our hearts this Advent, that we too may be *full of grace* by the power of the Holy Spirit.

O Mary, conceived without sin, pray for us who have recourse to thee.

Our Lady of Guadalupe

Today, in the heart of the Advent season, we celebrate the radiant Feast of Our Lady of Guadalupe, the "Patroness of the Americas" and the Mother of the True God for whom we live. This feast, so dear to the peoples of Mexico and to all the Americas, invites us to contemplate the Virgin Mary's maternal presence among the poor and lowly, and her mission of bearing Christ to the world.

It is no coincidence that the Gospel today — Luke's account of the Annunciation — is one we just heard a few days ago on the Solemnity of the Immaculate Conception. The repetition is liturgically deliberate and spiritually rich. It reminds us that the Blessed Virgin Mary, in her sinlessness and fiat, is not only the chosen instrument of the Incarnation, but also the model of Advent faith — the one who waits, receives, and carries the Word of God with perfect trust.

In the Gospel, the angel Gabriel comes to Mary with a message that forever changed the world:

> "Rejoice, full of grace, the Lord is with you... You will conceive in your womb and bear a son, and you shall name him Jesus" (Luke 1:28, 31).

Mary's response, *"Be it done unto me according to your word,"* is the very heart of what it means to live in Advent hope. She becomes the first tabernacle of the New Covenant — and the first to prepare a place for Christ, not merely in her body, but in her heart.

So too did she prepare a place for Him in the New World, when she appeared in 1531 to Saint Juan Diego on the hill of Tepeyac.

There, Mary came not with thunder and majesty but with gentleness and tenderness. She spoke not in the language of imperial power but in the humble Nahuatl tongue of the indigenous poor. And yet, her message echoed the voice of Gabriel: *"Am I not here who am your Mother?"*

Her tilma, her miraculous image, was not merely a marvel for the senses but a theological icon: clothed with the sun, standing on the moon, pregnant with the Christ Child, her eyes looking down in humility. She came as the Woman of Revelation, but also as the Virgin of Nazareth, and the Mother of Advent.

The first reading from Zechariah proclaims:

"Sing and rejoice, O daughter Zion! See, I am coming to dwell among you, says the Lord" (Zech 2:14).

This promise is fulfilled in Christ — but Mary is the first fruit of that dwelling. She is Zion in person, the holy dwelling place of God. When Our Lady of Guadalupe appeared at Tepeyac, she fulfilled anew that prophecy for the Americas: she made the presence of the true God known in a land often dominated by idolatry and oppression.

The responsorial canticle from Judith, a heroine of Israel, finds its ultimate fulfillment in Mary:

"You are the highest honor of our race... your deed of hope will never be forgotten" (Judith 13:18–19).

Mary is the new Judith who crushes the head of the enemy not with the sword, but with the humility of her faith and the power of her Son. Our Lady of Guadalupe's appearance helped bring millions to the faith — not by coercion, but by conversion of heart.

During this Advent season, when we are preparing for the coming of Christ at Christmas and at the end of time, Our Lady of Guadalupe teaches us how to receive Him: with faith, simplicity, and courage. Her presence assures us that God comes to dwell with the lowly, to raise the poor, and to comfort the afflicted.

So let us draw near to Mary in this season. Let us, like Juan Diego, climb the hill in our hearts to meet her. And let us, like her, say *yes* to God — *fiat mihi secundum verbum tuum* — and bear Christ anew into our world.

Our Lady of Guadalupe, Empress of the Americas and Star of the New Evangelization, pray for us

Christmas

The poem is by English poet Mary Coleridge and is entitled *Salus Mundi*:

I saw a stable, low and very bare,
A little child in a manger.
The oxen knew Him, had Him in their care, To men He was a
*   stranger.*
The safety of the world was lying there, And the world's danger.

The key to everything I hope to offer you all this week can be summarized in one phrase: a baby changes everything. A baby changes everything. To help you understand this concept, I can share with you a story. I am the baby of the family and, to top it off, I was a surprise baby. I came around ten years after my brother, so, in a way I was raised with my much older sisters being like other mothers to me. I was given the nickname "baby Jesus" by my brother, who likes to joke that everything was so much better before I was born! I am told that I changed everything in the family, being the annoying and needy little brother that I am.

This baby, this newborn King whom we hail in the manger, he is a danger. He is a danger.

This child is dangerous because nothing is as lovable as a baby. Babies, by their nature, are cute and cuddly. It's as if they have a little something about them that makes people, especially women, want to take care of them and men want to protect them.

If these children were lovable, even more so must have been the most adorable Jesus. This little Lord Jesus, asleep in the hay, is dangerous. Why? Because if we take seriously what goes on in the Nativity, then our whole little world will have to change; the world as we know it will have to change' Think about it: in our fallen human condition, how do we know the world, in its fallen human state, in our fallen human nature: we know it as violent, filled with hatred, with anger and avarice, with lust, shame; a world of sin. This Earth is groaning under the weight of it all.

Blessed Jordan of Saxony entered the Dominican order in 1220 and became St Dominic's successor as Master of the order in 1222. He worked and travelled tirelessly in that task till his death by shipwreck in 1237. Blessed Diana d'Andalò was a close friend of St Dominic's and made her religious profession in his hands in 1219. Four years later (two years after his death) she established the Dominican convent for contemplative nuns in Bologna, under the auspices of Jordan, with whom she developed a warm friendship. His letters to her are among the most personal documents to survive from the order's early years, and a testament to warm and deep friendship among the saints. Here is one of them - a Christmas letter.

Paris 1229

Dear Diana,

> *I cannot find the time to write you the long letter your love would wish for and I would so gladly send. Nonetheless I do write,*

I send you a very little word, the Word made little in the crib, the Word who was made flesh for us, the Word of salvation and grace, of sweetness and glory, the Word who is good and gentle, Jesus Christ and him crucified, Christ raised up on the cross, raised in praise to the Father's right hand: to whom and in whom do you raise up your soul and find there your rest unending for ever and ever.

Read over that Word in your heart, turn it over in your mind, let it be sweet as honey on your lips; ponder it, dwell on it, that it may dwell with you and in you for ever.

There is another word that I send you, small and brief; my love, which will speak for me to your love in your heart and will content it. May this word too be yours, and likewise dwell with you for ever.

Farewell, and pray for me,
Jordan

Into the darkness comes this very little word, this logos, the light of the world. We have the God of paradox present in our midst. God, all powerful, becomes all weak as a baby; God, all wise, becomes all needy, as a baby; God, who is eternal, enters into time as a baby. And he does this, all the while remaining God.

God becomes Incarnate. One of the classes I would love to create, and I know it sounds crazy, would be the Christology of Christmas Carols. Listen to the words of "Hark the Herald Angel Sing," written by Charles Wesley:

Hark the herald angels sing "Glory to the newborn King!
Peace on earth and mercy mild God and sinners reconciled"
Joyful, all ye nations rise Join the triumph of the skies With
the angelic host proclaim: "Christ is born in Bethlehem"
Hark! The herald angels sing "Glory to the newborn King!"
Christ by highest heav'n adored Christ the everlasting Lord!
Late in time behold Him come Offspring of a Virgin's womb
Veiled in flesh the Godhead see Hail the incarnate Deity
Pleased as man with man to dwell Jesus, our Emmanuel
Hark! The herald angels sing "Glory to the newborn King!"
Hail the heav'n-born Prince of Peace! Hail the Son of Right-
eousness! Light and life to all He brings Ris'n with healing in
His wings Mild He lays His glory by Born that man no more
may die Born to raise the sons of earth Born to give them
second birth Hark! The herald angels sing "Glory to the new-
born King!"

The incarnate God: God becomes one like us in all things but sin. "Nothing human is foreign to him." He knows our pain, our fear, our suffering. He who did not know sin becomes sin itself.

The same Christ who is born in the wood of the manger, poor and naked, wrapped in cloths, is the same Christ who died on the wood of the Cross, poor and naked, bloodied, "cursed, defiled, bruised, defiled," as the *Stabat Mater* reminds us.

This child, born to us, unto us a Son is given, is a promise and a pledge, but also a challenge.

Feast of the Holy Family
(Octave of Christmas)

On this Feast of the Holy Family—nestled within the Octave of Christmas—the Church proclaims something both simple and astonishing: we are saved through family. Not in the sentimental sense of a Hallmark card, but in the hard, costly, incarnational way God actually chooses to work in history.

The God revealed in Jesus Christ is not a distant architect who sets the universe in motion and steps back. He is not only Creator, but Sustainer—present, involved, patient. He acts *incarnationally*. And that means: He acts through families.

From the very beginning of salvation history, God binds His covenant to households and lineages—often messy, fractured, imperfect ones:

- Adam and Eve, and the tragic rupture between Cain and Abel
- Noah and his sons, through whom the world is preserved
- Abraham and Sarah, with Ishmael and Isaac, and then Jacob and Rebekah
- Joseph and his brothers, a family torn apart and yet reconciled by providence
- Moses, Aaron, and Miriam, siblings called together into God's saving work
- David and his sons, a royal family marked by greatness and grave sin

And finally, at the center of all history, the Holy Family—Jesus, Mary, and Joseph—alongside Zechariah and Elizabeth, and even Joachim and Anne, whose quiet fidelity prepared the way for the Mother of God.

God does not bypass family life to redeem the world. He enters it. He sanctifies it from the inside.

St. Matthew's Gospel places the Holy Family in stark contrast to another "family": the Herods.

Herod the Great—and the Herodian dynasty that followed him—were not legitimate kings of Israel. They were Idumeans, installed and sustained by Roman power, ruling through fear, violence, and political calculation. This was a family marked not by covenant but by paranoia: fathers murdering sons, brothers eliminating brothers, power preserved through bloodshed.

Herod's slaughter of the Holy Innocents is not an aberration; it is the logical fruit of a family—and a regime—built on self-preservation rather than self-gift.

Against this stands the Holy Family: powerless, displaced, forced into exile. One family clings to control and destroys life; the other entrusts itself to God and protects Life Himself.

At the heart of the Holy Family is trust.

Consider St. Joseph. The angel does not speak to him publicly or dramatically, but in dreams—the language of quiet obedience. Joseph never speaks a recorded word in Scripture, yet his actions speak volumes. He trusts, he rises, he takes the Child and His Mother, he flees, he returns. Again and again, he entrusts his life to God without full understanding.

Mary, however, encounters the angel differently. Gabriel speaks to her directly, face to face. The Church has always understood this as fitting, because Mary is the Immaculate Conception—untainted by sin, fully receptive to divine speech. Where Joseph listens in the shadows of sleep, Mary receives the Word in luminous clarity.

Different roles. Different graces. The same radical trust.

This is an important word for families today: holiness does not require identical paths, but shared obedience.

Finally, St. Thomas Aquinas helps us understand what sustains family life—not emotion alone, but love rightly understood.

For Aquinas, love is not first a feeling. Love is an act of the will: to will the good of the other. This is why he insists on the crucial distinction between loving someone and liking them.

You do not always like your spouse, your child, your parent, your sibling. Liking is emotional, spontaneous, changeable. But love—true love—is stable, chosen, sacrificial. It seeks the *authentic good* of the other, even when that good is costly to oneself.

This is the love St. Paul describes in Colossians: "Put on heartfelt compassion, kindness, humility, gentleness, and patience… bearing with one another and forgiving one another."

That is family love. That is the love through which God saves.

The Feast of the Holy Family reminds us that salvation does not descend from heaven fully formed and untouched by human complexity. It comes to us wrapped in swaddling clothes, entrusted to a mother and a foster father, carried across borders, tested by fear, sustained by trust, and held together by love.

God saves the world through families—including yours and mine.

May the Holy Family teach us to trust, to love beyond liking, and to become—however imperfectly—places where God continues His saving work.

Second Sunday of Christmas

"And the Word became flesh and dwelt among us." (John 1:14)

Today's Gospel takes us back to the Prologue of John, that majestic hymn which echoes Genesis itself: *"In the beginning was the Word, and the Word was with God, and the Word was God."* With these words, Saint John does not merely open a narrative; he opens a mystery—the mystery of God's eternal Word made flesh, the Incarnation, the heart of the Christmas season and indeed of all Christian faith.

We are now past the Nativity scene, the angel choirs, the shepherds, and even the Magi soon to arrive. And yet, the Church, in her wisdom, gives us this Sunday to reflect on what Christmas truly means—not simply sentiment, but theological reality: *Verbum caro factum est*—"the Word became flesh."

Our first reading from Sirach 24 gives poetic voice to divine Wisdom, personified as one who comes forth from the mouth of the Most High and pitches her tent among God's people. The early Church Fathers saw in this passage a foreshadowing of Christ, the Logos, who came to dwell not in a metaphorical tent, but in true human flesh, and pitched His tent—His tabernacle—among us.

As Saint Augustine says, *"He came in such a way that, remaining what He was, He became what He was not."* (Sermon 186) That is, Christ remained fully God and became fully man. In this mystery, God has not merely visited humanity—He has wedded Himself to it in the most intimate union imaginable.

Saint John tells us, *"From his fullness we have all received, grace upon grace."* (John 1:16) What is this "grace upon grace"? Saint

43

Thomas Aquinas explains that it refers to grace succeeding grace, the Old Covenant being fulfilled and surpassed in the New Covenant by the gift of divine life through Jesus Christ (cf. *Summa Theologiae*, III, q. 1, a. 2).

This is not a replacement but a fulfillment. The Law, as Saint John says, was given through Moses, but grace and truth came through Jesus Christ. The Law prepared, pointed, and promised; Christ embodies the promise and bestows the reality. What was once written on tablets of stone is now written on our hearts by the Spirit of the Son (cf. CCC 1965–1974).

Saint Paul, in the second reading from Ephesians, prays that "the eyes of your hearts may be enlightened" (Eph 1:18). This is no metaphorical flourish. It is a spiritual necessity. Without the light of Christ, our vision remains dim, our hearts closed, and our faith shallow.

The mystery of the Incarnation demands more than admiration—it demands contemplation, conversion, and discipleship. If Christ has truly become flesh, then nothing is merely mundane. Every moment, every sorrow, every joy, every suffering can now be united to the divine. Christ is Emmanuel—God with us—in every hospital room, every lonely home, every suffering soul.

Let us not pass too quickly from this season. The Word made flesh still dwells among us, above all in the Eucharist. As Pope Saint Leo the Great preached: *"What was visible in our Savior has passed over into His sacraments."* (Sermon 74.2) The same Word who was laid in a manger is now laid upon our altars. The same flesh which Mary held in her arms is now given to us under the veil of bread and wine.

Do we approach Him with awe, with reverence, with hunger and love?

As the world packs away decorations and resumes its routines, the Church proclaims: *"The Word became flesh and dwelt among us."* This is not the end of a season—it is the beginning of a new way of seeing, of living, of loving.

May we receive the Word, not just into our minds, but into our hearts and lives. May we live, as Saint Paul exhorts, as those who have been blessed in Christ with every spiritual blessing in the heavens (Eph 1:3). And may our lives be a tabernacle in which the Incarnate Word continues to dwell and be seen by the world.

O come, let us adore Him—Christ the Lord

Solemnity of Mary, Mother of God

On this Octave Day of Christmas, as the world celebrates a new calendar year, the Church celebrates Mary — the Mother of God (*Theotokos*) — and places before us the mystery of the Incarnation, in which time and eternity met in the womb of a virgin. We begin the new year by contemplating not merely the turning of a page, but the mystery of divine maternity, in which God became man and entered into our history through the obedience and faith of the Blessed Virgin Mary.

The title *Mother of God* does not exaggerate Mary's importance; rather, it protects the truth about Jesus Christ. As St. Cyril of Alexandria taught at the Council of Ephesus in 431,

"If anyone does not confess that Emmanuel is truly God, and therefore that the holy Virgin is the Mother of God (Theotokos), for she bore in the flesh the Word of God made flesh—let him be anathema."

This is not just piety; it is doctrine. The Catechism of the Catholic Church reaffirms:

"From the most ancient times the Blessed Virgin has been honored with the title of 'Mother of God'… to confess that Jesus is truly God and truly man" (*CCC* §495).

Mary is Mother of God not because she is the source of Christ's divinity, but because the one she bore in her womb is a divine Person, the eternal Son, now incarnate.

The Second Reading from St. Paul's Letter to the Galatians is dense with theological insight and deserves close attention:

"When the fullness of time had come, God sent his Son, born of a woman, born under the law, to ransom those under the law, so that we might receive adoption as sons" (Gal 4:4–5).

This is Paul's only direct reference to Mary, and he does so not to develop Mariology but to teach Christology and soteriology — that our redemption depends on the true humanity of the Son of God. The phrase *"born of a woman"* is deliberate: it is the human birth of the divine Son that makes us sons in Him.

St. Thomas Aquinas, in his *Commentary on Galatians*, explains that this verse shows both the eternity of the Son ("God sent His Son") and the reality of the Incarnation ("born of a woman"). It is, Aquinas says, the mystery of divine condescension: *"God became man so that man might become God, not by nature but by adoption."*

Furthermore, "born under the law" signifies not merely cultural context but the Son's full assumption of our condition. He submitted to the Law to fulfill and transcend it, to set us free from its curse.

The goal of this mission is crystal clear: adoption. As Paul writes, "so that we might receive adoption as sons." This is not merely a metaphor but a real participation in divine filiation. The Catechism notes, "Through Baptism, the Christian is sacramentally assimilated to Jesus… making him a 'son' in the Son" (*CCC* §1272).

And Paul concludes: *"So you are no longer a slave but a son, and if a son then also an heir, through God."*

This is the dignity of the Christian: no longer outside the household, but made co-heirs with Christ.

Today's Gospel from Luke 2 recounts the visit of the shepherds to the newborn Christ. The humble men of the fields come in haste and return glorifying God — but Mary, the Gospel says, "kept all these things, reflecting on them in her heart" (Luke 2:19).

This phrase echoes the contemplative heart of Mary, who, as St. Bernard of Clairvaux wrote, *"conceived Christ in her heart by faith before she conceived Him in her womb."* Mary does not merely receive the Word once. She continues to ponder, to let the mystery unfold in silence, modeling the interior li   fe of the Church.

Moreover, on this day, Jesus is named — *Jesus,* which means "God saves" — and He is circumcised, signifying His full incorporation into Israel. St. Augustine notes, "Though the Word could not be bound by the Law, He subjected Himself to it to fulfill righteousness for our sake."

As we begin this new civil year, the Church entrusts us to Mary's maternal care. The first reading from Numbers gives us the ancient priestly blessing, which the Church now places on Mary's lips for us:

"The LORD bless you and keep you! The LORD let His face shine upon you and be gracious to you!" (Num 6:24–25).

Through Mary, God's face has shone upon us, literally — in the face of the Christ Child.

Let us not enter this new year with resolutions of our own strength alone. Let us enter it under the mantle of Mary, the Mother of God, who bore the Prince of Peace, and who intercedes for us still. She who gave us Christ once in the flesh now prays that He may be born in our hearts by grace.

O Mary, Mother of God, pray for us sinners now and at the hour of our death. Amen.

Epiphany

Today we celebrate the Solemnity of the Epiphany, the "manifestation" of Jesus Christ to the nations. While the world may see Epiphany as the end of the Christmas season, for the Church, Epiphany is the culmination and fulfillment of Christmas. The newborn King who was revealed to the humble shepherds of Israel is now unveiled to the Gentile world in the persons of the Magi. As Saint Leo the Great preached in the 5th century: *"A star led the Magi to adore Jesus, the star of Jacob, and thus the faith of all nations began to shine forth."*

Christmas is the mystery of the Word made flesh, but Epiphany is the mystery of the Word revealed to the world. It is the universal expansion of the Incarnation — Christ is not only the Messiah of Israel but the Savior of all peoples. The Church Fathers often referred to this day as the "theophany" — the revelation of God's glory to the Gentiles.

The Gospel of Matthew tells us of Magi — wise men from the East — who were drawn by the light of a star to find the newborn King of the Jews. But they are more than exotic visitors; they are the first fruits of the Gentiles, the foreshadowing of the universal Church. As St. Augustine wrote: *"The Magi were the first to proclaim the Gospel to the Gentiles, by adoring Christ."* (*Sermon 200.3*)

The first reading from Isaiah 60 rings out with triumph: *"Nations shall walk by your light, and kings by your shining radiance… they shall bring gold and frankincense, and proclaim the praises of the Lord."*

Isaiah's words are fulfilled not only in the journey of the Magi, but in the mission of the Church: to draw all nations into the light of Christ.

The Church Fathers saw this as the fulfillment of God's promise to Abraham — that all the nations would be blessed through his seed.

Psalm 72 also echoes this universal vision: *"May all kings fall down before him, all nations serve him."*

The gifts of gold, frankincense, and myrrh offered by the Magi are not just valuable — they are symbolic of Christ's identity, namely, gold for His kingship, frankincense for His divinity, and myrrh for His sacrificial death

As St. Gregory the Great teaches: *"The Magi's gifts signify the mystery of who this Child is: gold for the King, frankincense for God, and myrrh for the one who will die."*

Saint Paul in the second reading from Ephesians reveals the full depth of the Epiphany mystery: *"The Gentiles are coheirs, members of the same body, and copartners in the promise in Christ Jesus through the Gospel"* (Eph 3:6).

Here, the hidden plan of God is now made known: salvation is not reserved for a particular people but is open to all. The Church is catholic — universal — because Christ came for all, and the Epiphany is the day that universality dawns.

This liturgical feast is more than a historical commemoration. It is a proclamation of the Church's missionary identity. The same Christ whom the Magi sought under a star is the Christ we adore in the Eucharist and proclaim to the world. The Magi came to worship — so must we. They returned home by another way — and so must we, transformed by our encounter with the Savior.

Culturally, Epiphany is one of the most significant Christian celebrations throughout the world. In the East, it traditionally marked the celebration of Christ's Baptism. In Spain and Latin America, it is often called *El Día de los Reyes*, the Day of the Kings — a time of gift-giving, celebration, and devotion. In places like Italy, children receive gifts not on December 25 but on January 6. In the liturgical tradition, this feast has been known as the "Second Christmas," especially in the East and in ancient Rome.

The Epiphany reminds us that Christianity is not a private or tribal faith, but a cosmic and global one. The same Child who lay in a manger is Lord of every people, every land, every heart.

Let us not forget the spiritual response of the Magi: they fell down and worshipped Him. Their journey ends not in speculation, but in adoration. And as St. John Chrysostom noted: "They came and worshipped Him, offering gifts, gold, frankincense, and myrrh; showing by their gifts that they acknowledged Him to be both King, God, and Man who should die."

— *Homily VI on Matthew* (§6; PG 57:65).

Brothers and sisters, this Epiphany, may we be like the Magi — those who search for Christ, follow the light, and give Him everything. May our hearts be the treasures we lay before Him.

Arise, shine, for your light has come, and the glory of the Lord has risen upon you.

The Baptism of the Lord

Today, with the Feast of the Baptism of the Lord, we conclude the liturgical season of Christmas and enter into Ordinary Time. And yet, this feast is not an afterthought. It is, in fact, the third great Epiphany — after the Magi's adoration and the wedding at Cana — wherein the identity of Jesus is publicly manifested, now at the Jordan River.

At first glance, today's Gospel is puzzling. Jesus, the sinless Son of God, comes to John to receive a baptism of repentance. Even John is confused: *"I need to be baptized by you, and yet you are coming to me?"* (Matt 3:14)

Why would Christ, who is without sin — as the Church teaches clearly — submit Himself to a baptism meant for sinners? Saint Thomas Aquinas addresses this very question in the *Summa Theologiae (ST III, q. 39, a. 1)*. He writes that Jesus was baptized, not to be cleansed Himself, but: *"to sanctify the waters, so that they might have the power to cleanse others."*

In other words, Christ entered the waters not to be made holy, but to make them holy. His descent into the Jordan is a prelude to the Cross: the sinless One identifying Himself with sinners, descending into our condition so that we might rise with Him. It is also, Aquinas notes, a manifestation of humility, fulfilling the words of Isaiah from today's first reading: *"He shall not cry out, nor shout, nor make his voice heard in the street... a bruised reed he shall not break."*(Isaiah 42:2–3) Christ reveals His glory not in thunderous self-assertion, but in solidarity with the lowly.

The Church Fathers viewed the Baptism of Jesus as a profound moment of theophany — the manifestation of the Holy Trinity. The voice of the Father is heard: *"This is my beloved Son"*. The Son is present in the flesh. The Spirit descends like a dove. As Saint Gregory of Nazianzus wrote:

"Let us be cleansed and let us put on new garments, not such as are soiled again, but that we may be made whiter and brighter. Let us honor Christ's Baptism and celebrate this feast in holiness. Be cleansed entirely and continue to be cleansed. Nothing gives so much pleasure to God as the conversion and salvation of man. The heavens, as it were, open again, and the Spirit bears witness to His Godhead, for He comes down in the form of a dove and brings honor to the body, since He is God and of God." (Oration 39, *On the Holy Lights*, §§14–15.)

Thus, the Baptism of the Lord is not a private act of devotion, but the re-creation of the world in sacramental form. Just as the Spirit hovered over the waters in Genesis, now the Spirit hovers over the waters of the Jordan, inaugurating the new creation in Christ.

What, then, does this feast teach us about our own baptism? As the Catechism of the Catholic Church affirms: "Through Baptism we are freed from sin and reborn as sons of God; we become members of Christ, are incorporated into the Church and made sharers in her mission." (*CCC* §1213)

Christ's baptism is the prototype and source of ours. In it, He opens the path by which we are united to His Passion, death, and Resurrection — what St. Paul calls "dying and rising with Christ" (cf. Rom 6:3–5). And as Acts 10 reveals, through Christ and the baptism He institutes, *"God shows no partiality... everyone who fears Him and acts uprightly is acceptable to Him.*" This universal call to salvation reaches its sacramental beginning in the waters of baptism.

We must not miss the deep liturgical connection between today's feast and the Epiphany. In many Eastern Churches, the Baptism of the Lord is the primary celebration of Epiphany, because it is here that Christ is revealed not only to a few wise men, but to the whole of Israel, gathered at the Jordan.

The Church's liturgy captures this connection. The Antiphon for the Benedictus today reads: *"Today the heavens opened and the waters were sanctified; the earth rejoices, and the angels marvel, for Christ is baptized by John in the Jordan."*

Thus, today's feast is not merely the end of Christmas — it is the unveiling of Christ's mission. The Child of Bethlehem now steps into public ministry. The star of the Magi gives way to the voice from heaven. The swaddling clothes are replaced by the flowing waters of the Jordan.

As we enter Ordinary Time, the Baptism of the Lord reminds us that our lives are anything but ordinary when lived in the grace of our own baptism. It is the beginning of our Christian vocation, our share in Christ's priestly, prophetic, and kingly mission.

The Psalm today proclaims: *"The Lord will bless His people with peace."*

That blessing began in Christ's baptism and reaches each of us through the sacrament we have received. Let us renew our baptismal promises not merely with words, but with lives lived in holiness, charity, and mission. Let us marvel at the humility of Christ, the sinless One who enters the waters for us. Let us adore the Trinity revealed on this day. And let us live out the grace of our baptism —

daily dying to sin, daily rising with Christ, daily walking as beloved sons and daughters of the Father.

Saint Thomas Aquinas, with his usual clarity, reminds us: *"The baptism of Christ was the consecration of baptism."* (*ST III, q. 39, a. 1 ad 1*) May we who have received this consecration walk in the light of the beloved Son.

Ash Wednesday

Today we begin the holy and penitential season of Lent, and we do so with the solemn rites and readings of Ash Wednesday, a day heavy with symbolism, yet full of hope. In every corner of the world today, Catholics will hear the ancient words, *"Remember you are dust, and to dust you shall return,"* and feel the gritty ashes traced upon their foreheads. This is no empty ritual; it is the beginning of a sacred journey — a journey that draws its deepest inspiration from Scripture, Tradition, and the lived practice of the Church through the centuries.

At the heart of today's liturgy is the piercing call of the prophet Joel: *"Even now, says the Lord, return to me with your whole heart, with fasting, weeping, and mourning. Rend your hearts, not your garments."* (Joel 2:12–13)

These words, spoken in the midst of a national crisis in ancient Israel, are not merely historical. They are addressed to us, here and now, as we face our own crises — spiritual, cultural, personal. Joel doesn't call for superficial reform but a radical interior conversion: not torn clothes, but torn hearts. This is a call to interior transformation — what the Fathers of the Church often referred to as *metanoia*, a change of mind and heart.

Saint Cyprian of Carthage, writing in the third century, taught: *"Let us repent with our whole heart. Let us return to the Lord with tears and groaning, as He Himself commands... asking forgiveness with fasting and sackcloth."* (*De Lapsis*, 32)

Joel's vision of communal repentance, including the priests, the ministers, the elders, and even the bride and bridegroom, reveals that no one is exempt from this call to conversion. And the context of the passage — the *Day of the Lord* — connects Lent with the urgency of salvation. As Saint Paul echoes in today's epistle: *"Now is the acceptable time; now is the day of salvation."* (2 Cor 6:2)

The season of Lent has its roots in the earliest centuries of the Church as a time of preparation for baptism at Easter. Originally, it was primarily for catechumens — those preparing to enter the Church — but soon all Christians were invited to join in a 40-day period of prayer, fasting, and almsgiving, imitating Christ's forty days in the wilderness.

The 40-day structure was formalized by the Council of Nicaea in 325 A.D. By the seventh century, Roman Christians began the practice of marking the beginning of Lent with ashes, drawing from Old Testament penitential customs. Tertullian refers to wearing sackcloth and ashes as acts of *exomologesis* — public confession and penance.

Ash Wednesday itself appears in the Roman liturgy by the 11th century, when Pope Urban II officially made it the start of Lent. The imposition of ashes is deeply biblical — a sign of mourning, mortality, and repentance. Job repents *"in dust and ashes"* (Job 42:6); Daniel pleads with God in *"prayer and fasting and sackcloth and ashes"* (Dan 9:3).

Yet even this outward sign must be grounded in interior renewal, as Jesus teaches in today's Gospel. Jesus warns us not to make our fasting and prayer a performance: *"When you give alms, do not blow a trumpet... When you fast, do not look gloomy."* He's not discouraging prayer, fasting, or almsgiving — quite the opposite. He's calling us to make them authentic, performed not for human approval, but out of love for the Father who *"sees in secret."*

Saint Augustine, commenting on this passage, explains:

"Do not let your left hand know what your right hand is doing — that is, do not let your intention for praise come in between your action and God, to whom you should look for your reward."

— *St. Augustine, Sermon 56, §10.*

And again, later in the same homily (§11):

"Let your right hand do good works, and let not your left hand know — that is, do not let your desire for human praise mingle with your good work. Seek the reward from your Father, who sees in secret."

Lent is a season of hidden growth — like seeds buried in the soil — nourished by secret acts of love, quiet sacrifices, and renewed prayer.

The Responsorial Psalm, Psalm 51, gives us the Church's Lenten anthem: *"Create in me a clean heart, O God."* It reminds us that Lent is not about self-improvement or self-denial for its own sake. It is about grace. It is about letting God create anew in us a heart that is ready to love, to serve, and to be reconciled.

And how timely Joel's words are for us this year: *"Return to me with your whole heart."* In a time of spiritual distraction, division, and disillusionment — both in the world and at times even within the Church — we are being invited back to the essentials: prayer, repentance, worship, humility.

We begin this season not in despair, but in hope. Joel concludes with a word of consolation: *"Who knows? He may again relent and leave behind a blessing."* (Joel 2:14)

Lent does not end in ashes. It ends in fire — the fire of Easter, when Christ rises victorious, and we, renewed, rise with Him.

Let this Lent be for each of us a true return. Let us rend our hearts and not just our garments. Let us fast, not to impress others, but to make room for God. Let us pray, not out of obligation, but because we long to speak with our Father. Let us give alms, not to soothe our conscience, but to open our hearts.

This Lent, "now is the acceptable time." Let us rise from ashes, and walk toward the Paschal dawn.

First Sunday of Lent

On this First Sunday of Lent, the Church sets before us the great drama of salvation that begins in a garden and leads into a desert: from Adam's temptation in Eden to Christ's victory in the wilderness. These readings are not mere stories from the past — they speak to the deepest realities of our own human condition, and the divine remedy God has wrought through Jesus Christ, the New Adam.

We begin with Genesis 2 and 3, which recount the mysterious but foundational truth of original sin. God forms Adam from the dust of the ground and breathes into him the breath of life. He is placed in Eden, given freedom, and entrusted with a command. But through the cunning of the serpent and the seduction of pride, Adam and Eve reach for what was not theirs — the knowledge of good and evil, on their own terms.

As the Catechism of the Catholic Church explains: *"Man, tempted by the devil, let his trust in his Creator die in his heart and, abusing his freedom, disobeyed God's command. This is what man's first sin consisted of."* (CCC §397)

This disobedience ruptures the original harmony: between man and God, man and woman, man and creation, and even within the human heart itself. From this wound arises concupiscence — our disordered desires. Saint Augustine famously called it the "massa damnata" — the mass of damnation — from which only grace can redeem us.

As Psalm 51 echoes: *"In sin my mother conceived me... a clean heart create for me, O God."* We are not born evil, but we are born wounded — in need of a Savior.

In Matthew 4, Jesus is led by the Spirit into the wilderness to be tempted by the devil. Here we must pause. Why would Jesus, the sinless Son of God, be tempted? Can God be tempted? And if He cannot sin, what is the meaning of this confrontation?

Saint Thomas Aquinas addresses this in his *Summa Theologiae* (*ST III, q. 41, a.1*). He explains that Christ's temptation was not for His sake, but for ours:

"Christ willed to be tempted:

> *(1) That He might strengthen us against temptation by His example.*
> *(2) That we might have confidence in His mercy.*
> *(3) That He might overcome the tempter on our behalf."*

Though Christ, as the divine Person, could not sin, He allowed Himself to experience real temptation in His human nature — not to struggle as we do in weakness, but to confront and defeat the devil as the New Adam. Where the first Adam fell amid abundance, Christ triumphed amid hunger.

And note well the threefold pattern of the temptations:

1. "Turn these stones to bread" — a temptation to bodily satisfaction apart from the will of God.
2. "Throw yourself down" — a temptation to pride and presumption, using God for self-glory.
3. "All these kingdoms I will give you" — a temptation to idolatry, to power without the Cross.

These mirror the temptations described by 1 John 2:16: *"the lust of the flesh, the lust of the eyes, and the pride of life."*

The Fathers of the Church, especially St. Irenaeus, saw in these temptations a reverse of Eden: *"As Eve was seduced by the word of an angel [the fallen one] to flee from God, so Mary received glad tidings from the angel to bear God. Thus, by the obedience of one, the disobedience of the other was undone."* (*Adversus Haereses* V.19.1)

So too in Christ's desert victory, the disobedience of Adam is reversed. Christ is victorious not merely as an example but as our Redeemer — He conquers sin on our behalf.

This Sunday marks our own entry into the Lenten desert, a sacred time to confront our temptations, to recognize our frailty, and to rediscover the grace of our baptismal identity. As Saint Paul writes in Romans 5, *"Through one man sin entered the world... but much more did the grace of God and the gift of the one man Jesus Christ overflow to the many."*

In Christ, we have not just a second chance — we have a new nature, begun in baptism and nourished through the sacraments.

The Catechism reminds us: *"By the grace of baptism, all sins are forgiven, original sin and all personal sins, as well as all punishment for sin."* (CCC §1263) Yet this grace must be lived. Lent is not a time of mere self-discipline, but of conversion — of turning from self to God, from appetite to adoration, from pride to penance.

The first Sunday of Lent reminds us of who we are — sons and daughters of Adam, wounded by sin — and who we are called to become — sons and daughters of God, healed by Christ.

Let us follow Christ into the desert. Let us fast, pray, and resist temptation not by our own strength, but by the Word of God. Let us allow this Lent to be a time not of mere obligation, but of renewal — a time to rend our hearts and return to the Lord.

And let us remember: the desert is not the end. Christ's victory over Satan here foreshadows His greater victory over sin and death on the Cross. Lent is a journey to Easter — and today, Christ leads the way.

Second Sunday of Lent

Each year on the Second Sunday of Lent, the Church places before us the radiant mystery of the Transfiguration of the Lord — a moment of divine glory shining forth in the midst of Christ's journey toward Jerusalem and the Cross. This is no accident. The Transfiguration is not a detour from Lent's theme of penance and self-denial — it is its illumination. Today, the Church reminds us that glory can only come through suffering, and that our Lenten journey must be animated by the theological virtue of hope.

The Gospel from Matthew 17 recounts how Jesus takes Peter, James, and John up the high mountain and is transfigured before them. His face shines like the sun, and His garments become white as light. He stands in conversation with Moses and Elijah — the Law and the Prophets — and the voice of the Father thunders, *"This is my beloved Son... listen to Him."*

This moment, as St. Leo the Great writes, is not merely for Christ's sake but for ours:

"The principal aim of the Transfiguration was to remove the scandal of the cross from the hearts of His disciples... so that the humiliation of the Passion might not disturb the faith of those who had seen the splendor of His hidden majesty." (Sermon 51 on the Transfiguration)

The Transfiguration is the epiphany of hope — a foretaste of resurrection glory. And yet it comes before the Passion, not after. Jesus is preparing His disciples for the dark valley ahead by showing them the summit that awaits.

St. Thomas Aquinas in his *Summa Theologiae* (*ST III, q. 45*) teaches that Christ was transfigured for several reasons:

1. To confirm the faith of the apostles before His Passion.
2. To reveal the glory of the resurrection promised to all the faithful.
3. To teach us that the way to glory is through suffering — that one must be configured to the Cross in order to share in the Crown.

Aquinas draws a connection between this event and the virtue of hope, for it is hope that sustains the soul amid trial, keeping it oriented toward the glory to come.

The Church gives us Lent not as a season of despair, but as a season of hope-filled discipline. We do not fast as those who seek death, but as those who long for eternal life. As St. Paul reminds us in today's second reading: *"Bear your share of hardship for the Gospel... with the strength that comes from God. He saved us and called us to a holy life... now made manifest through the appearance of our Savior Christ Jesus."* (2 Timothy 1:8–10)

This is the virtue of hope — a trust in God's promises, grounded not in our own strength, but in the grace given to us "before time began," now revealed in Christ.

As the Catechism of the Catholic Church explains:

"Hope is the theological virtue by which we desire the kingdom of heaven and eternal life as our happiness... placing our trust in Christ's promises and relying not on our own strength, but on the help of the grace of the Holy Spirit." (CCC §1817)

Lent is the gymnasium of hope. By prayer, fasting, and almsgiving, we retrain our desires toward what is eternal. We learn to carry the cross — not with stoicism, but with expectation.

The first reading from Genesis recounts how God calls Abram to leave behind everything — his country, his kin, his father's house — and set out into the unknown. All he has is God's promise: *"I will bless you... and through you all the families of the earth shall be blessed."*

Abram's journey is the model of faith and the prototype of Christian hope. He walks into the unknown because he trusts the One who has called him. Just so, we begin Lent in the darkness of the desert — and like Abram, we walk not by sight, but by trust in the One who goes before us.

As St. Augustine says: "Our whole life is a journey of faith; as long as we are on pilgrimage away from the Lord, we walk by faith and not by sight." — *Sermon 234, On the Anniversary of a Bishop's Ordination, §3.*

Peter's instinct at the Transfiguration is to stay — to build tents and remain in the glory. But Jesus leads them down the mountain, back to the journey, back to the Cross. And He does the same with us.

Every Lent we ascend the mountain of prayer, fasting, and almsgiving. But it is not to escape suffering — it is to be strengthened to face it with renewed purpose. The Cross is not the end. As the Psalm today reminds us: *"See, the eyes of the Lord are upon those who fear Him, upon those who hope for His kindness."* (Psalm 33:18)

Let us this Lent follow Jesus up the mountain. Let us behold His glory in prayer, embrace His path in penance, and renew our hope in His promise.

Because the Transfiguration teaches us this: the path to glory is the path of the Cross. And Lent is not a detour — it is the way.

"Listen to Him," the Father says. Let us listen — in Scripture, in silence, in suffering — and know that He leads us not to despair, but to transfiguration.

Third Sunday of Lent

Our Lord Jesus' encounter with the Samaritan woman, who is simply looking for some water, is a supreme example of what Pope Francis calls "accompaniment." The Pope in his apostolic exhortation *Evangelii Gaudium* (169) describes accompaniment as an art, a skill. He states: "The Church will have to initiate everyone — priests, religious and laity —into this 'art of accompaniment' which teaches us to remove our sandals before the sacred ground of the other (cf. Ex 3:5)."

Jesus, in the Gospel, meets the woman where she is at; and, where she is at is, literally, the well. She is there simply looking to fetch a pail of water. And the Lord Jesus — he who is all truth — meets her there and leads her gently, patiently, to truth. Notice that it is the Lord himself who initiates conversation with her. He, a devout Jew, deigns to speak to a Samaritan — one who is unclean by birth, a member of a sect of Judaism that had broken far away from the mainstream religion and married into foreigners. On top of that, Jesus is speaking to a woman. In those days, no man would speak in public to a strange woman, if both he and she were to be considered respectable.

Jesus asks her for some water. And this stops her in her tracks. He asks her to go out of herself, if only for a moment, and to enter into service. This is why true conversions of faith happen when we engage people in service projects, in helping the poor, for instance. In serving others we go from the natural level, from a natural desire to help others, to the supernatural level, of beginning to recognize Christ in the midst of the people we are serving. Think of all the vocations to priesthood and religious life that begin with service projects in the parish.

The Lord Jesus gradually engages this woman, meeting her where she is — and, through dialogue, patience, charity, and humility, he brings her to where she must be, namely, to friendship with himself. This is the art of accompaniment of which the pope speaks: "Genuine spiritual accompaniment always begins and flourishes in the context of service to the mission of evangelization" (*EG*, 173). The Pope explains further: "Spiritual accompaniment must lead others ever closer to God ... to accompany them would be counterproductive if it became a sort of therapy supporting their self-absorption and ceased to be a pilgrimage with Christ to the Father." (*EG*, 170)

This accompaniment is not about watering down the truth. The Lord Jesus, who knows the hearts of all, does not begin his conversation with this woman with a laundry list of her sins. He helps her understand her situation in life, her many sins. He helps her comprehend for the first time that she is truly thirsting for the water, the living water that only the Lord Jesus, who is life and truth, can give. It's in his dialogue with her that the Lord shows us the art of accompaniment. Pope Francis writes: "Listening, in communication, is an openness of heart which makes possible that closeness without which genuine spiritual encounter cannot occur" (*EG*, 171).

It's the job of priests and those involved in apostolic service to know what the Church teaches and to present it clearly. We have to model the truth of the faith by living it out daily. We can't water down the truth, especially about marriage, life issues (for nothing is more essential than the sanctity of life), the integrity of the sacraments (especially the Holy Eucharist), and issues of sexuality and gender. We have to know what the Church teaches and to be able to communicate it clearly and concisely.

Genuine encounter is born from a respectful attitude toward the other person, from a conviction that the other person has something good to say. It supposes that we can make room in our heart for their point of view, their opinion and their proposals. Dialogue entails a warm reception and not a preemptive condemnation. To dialogue, one must know how to lower the defenses, to open the doors of one's home and to offer warmth," as Pope Francis reminds us. True dialogue doesn't mean just smiling and listening, nodding along, and giving tacit approval. Nor does it mean simply lecturing another person. Jesus engages in dialogue, but he is pretty direct when it comes to the reality of the presence of sin in the woman's life. And yet, he who is mercy walks with her. What does this mean?

It means beginning on the natural level — and then moving to the supernatural level. Through the Spirit working in our midst, we go deeper and deeper to engage with another person not just on the level of emotions, and not just on the level of the intellect, but on the level of the soul. The Gospel of the woman at the well is a masterpiece of the art of accompaniment. The Lord Jesus meets her where she is and exposes her gradually to the truth without watering it down. And then, once she sees the truth and begins to embrace it, what does she do? She goes and brings others to see this man, the Lord Jesus, who knows everything about her. This art of accompaniment is a fine and necessary tool in the work of evangelization, and the encounter of Our Lord with the woman at the well is the supreme exemplification of the science of accompaniment.

Fourth Sunday of Lent

I recall being in fifth grade at Holy Name of Jesus School in Windsor Terrace when my teacher told my parents that I was having some problems reading what was written on the blackboard. My perceptive teacher noticed my squinting and my struggling to write down what was on the blackboard in that venerable grammar school, which is now known as Saint Joseph the Worker Catholic Academy. This would have been in 1982, a very long time ago.

My parents took me out to around Kings Plaza to a Cohen's Fashion Optical and I had my eyes tested. About a week later, my father took the ten-year-old me that I was out to the eyeglass store and I tried my eyeglasses on the first time. I vividly recall being able to see so much better; it was like a new world of details was opened before me which I had not realized was there.

As time went on, especially as I got into my teenage years, I tried to not wear my eyeglasses and, as one could imagine, the results were what you would expect- not really seeing what was in front of me, as I would wear my eyeglasses at home but not at Cathedral Prep in Elmhurst, where I went for high school. By my sophomore year, at the strong suggestion of my Principal, one of the kindest priests I have ever known (and if I had to put forward a saint whom I know, it would be he), I began to wear my eyeglasses, which I needed to wear daily. Sure, I tried contact lens as a newly ordained priest, but I found myself lost without my eyeglasses. To this date, with slightly over fifty years of life on Earth, the first thing I do in the morning when I rise to is grab my eyeglasses. I often think back to the very first time I tried on my first pair of eyeglasses, a little boy's brown (my mother's favorite color) plastic aviator frame, I felt like I could not only see, but actually perceive.

In today's readings from the Old Testament book of First Samuel and in the Holy Gospel according to Saint John, we read not only about seeing, but perhaps more importantly about perceiving. The great Roman Catholic apologist Bishop Robert E. Barron, in his masterpiece *And Now I See: A Theology of Transformation* (1998) states: "Christianity is, above all else, a way of seeing. Everything else in Christian life flows from and circles around the transformation of vision. Christians see differently, and that is why their prayer, their worship, their action, their whole way of being in in the world have a distinctive accent and flavor." (ix).

In the first reading taken from the First Book of the Prophet Samuel, we are placed in the midst of this drama to find a new king for the people of Israel. Recall that the Lord God did not want Israel to ever have a king, because he was the King of Israel. However, Israel wanted to have a king whom they could see, like the kings of other nations. The Lord God, again and again, stated that he did not want a visible King for Israel, because he is their king. In order to remind them of this fact, the Lord God set up Prophets, whose main role was to remind Israel that God and God alone is king.

Yes, the nation of Israel wanted a king whom they could see and the Lord God reminded them, time and again, that he is King and, if they choose earthly kings, things would go awry for them. Still, the nation of Israel, persisted and they had a king- Saul, who has some serious emotional problems, to say the least.

Into the picture comes the great prophet Samuel, who has to anoint a new king of Israel at the Lord's command. The only problem is that the Lord God has not told Samuel which of the sons of Jesse whom he should anoint.

As Jesse examines each son, he, as might we all in his case, sees some healthy, happy, holy young men, all of whom could easily be the next King of Israel. However, until he perceives, going beyond his mere sight, pushing beyond what is immediately presented in front of his sight, does he move beyond seeing and truly perceive who is really standing in front of him.

To the average eye, David is meek, small, young, and tiny. He is the "runt of the litter" and will win no "Mr. Universe" contests. David is a shepherd, a kid who takes care of the literal "kids," the sheep. In the eyes of the world, he has little value, compared to his heroic and confident brothers. And yet, in the eyes of the Lord, with which the Prophet Samuel is functioning, David is seen as he is- a human being created in God's image and likeness, one who, despite the presence of original sin, is still fundamentally good. Samuel is able to go beyond merely seeing, but actually to the level of perceiving who is really in front of him, namely the King of Israel.

In our lives, perhaps each of us needs to ask a simple question this Lent- do we see or do we perceive? Can we look at every single woman and man, every human person, whom we encounter and see them as they truly are- a beautifully created human being made in the image and likeness of God himself? Are we able to see each person whom we come across in our daily lives are fundamentally good and worthy of God's love, God's mercy, and God's forgiveness? And turning to the eyes of our Christian perception inwardly, are we able to see, no, truly perceive, the image and likeness of God, our loving Father and creator in ourselves?

This week, let us ask for the grace to not only see but to perceive who it is that is really in front of us. With each soul whom we encounter, we meet someone created in the image and likeness of Christ, and someone who is fundamentally good, despite the presence of original sin (which is washed away in the Sacrament of Baptism). Let's pray for the eyes of Samuel the Prophet, the eyes of Christ the healer, so that we can see the world as it truly is- the handiwork of God and each woman and man as the masterpiece of God's creation.

Fifth Sunday of Lent

When we encounter the Lord Jesus in today's Gospel, he is at his low point, at the nadir of his popularity when we encounter Him here. He's away from the main stage, away from Jerusalem. He received word that one of his closest friends, Lazarus, is dead. Jesus waits three days, foreshadowing the time He will spend in the tomb, before going to see Lazarus' sisters, Martha and Mary. The Lord loves these women. They are his friends and he delights in their company. He delays in his arrival outside of Bethany so that the glory of God can be shown. He finds his dear friends, these women whom he loves and who love him, weeping, with Martha, filled with confusion, yet with faith in the one she has come to know as God, confronts Him. Then we see Jesus at His most human, (recall the shortest verse in all of Scripture: "Jesus wept.") Jesus is sad, crying with and for Martha, Mary and His deceased friend, Lazarus. He is truly sorrowful, grieving in His human nature, but He does not despair.

We see the Lord Jesus at His most human in this Gospel, but then, suddenly we see Him at His most Divine. By His own power as divine, He raises the long dead, stinking, rotting Lazarus (remember the verse in the King James Version: "He stinketh.") from the dead. This was not just resuscitation; this was a resurrection. And this is the greatest sign of who Jesus is, the most undeniable proof of His Divine Sonship until He rises from the dead at Easter. What's the difference between the raising of Lazarus and the resurrection of Jesus? The Lord is raised to eternal life; Lazarus is raised to earthly life. Lazarus will die once more on earth, but the Lord Jesus will never die.

Jesus calls Lazarus out of the tomb, and we read that Lazarus comes out, bound hand and foot. The Lord says these simple words: "Untie him, and let him go free." A simple question- if he were bound, hand and foot, as the Gospel recounts, how then did he come out of the tomb? Did he hope? According to Saint Bernard, Lazarus just floated out. Regardless of that aside, Lazarus s raised to earthly life by the Lord Jesus as a foreshadowing of what will so soon occur to the Lord Jesus Himself.

With this in mind, what is the Lord Jesus saying to us today? The same Jesus, who is fully human and fully divine is calling to us, beckoning us to let Him untie us and to let us go free.

What's tying us up and refusing to let us go free? I'd venture to guess it is sin. Jesus wants us to be free from sin, so He offers us the beauty of the sacrament of penance, something of which we should all partake often, especially in these last days of Lent, as we venture onward towards Holy Week.

What tangling us in its web? What is ensnaring us in layers of linen that so binds us? Is it worry? Is it lack of knowledge of what will come next? Is it despair? We need a break, a day when we don't receive a gut punch, making us as a College, a Church, a world, fall to our knees gasping for breath.

It is Jesus alone who can heal us. Look to the fact that in March of 2020, the Holy Father, Pope Francis, in what many believe is his finest moment as the Supreme Pontiff, alone on a rainy, cold night in an empty piazza, one only a few weeks prior teeming with life, offered the greatest *Orbi et Urbi* of modern days- a blessing not from himself, as the Vicar of Christ on Earth, but from God HIMSELF, Christ, the Lord, truly present sacramentally in the Eucharist. Only

Jesus can make that first incision, only he holds the scissor. Jesus is there, loving us, gently unwrapping the layers that bind us and cause us not to live in the freedom of the sons and daughters of God. But we can help, too, once that first thread is pulled. This is our task now as brothers and sisters of Christ and of one another...

For those who enjoy the writings of J.R.R. Tolkien, I think that Samwise's encouragement to Frodo in *The Two Towers* is what we need to hear right now:

Frodo : I can't do this, Sam.

Sam : I know.

It's all wrong

By rights we shouldn't even be here.

But we are.

It's like in the great stories Mr. Frodo.

The ones that really mattered.

Full of darkness and danger they were,

and sometimes you didn't want to know the end.

Because how could the end be happy.

How could the world go back to the way it was when so much bad happened.

But in the end, it's only a passing thing, this shadow.

Even darkness must pass.

A new day will come.

And when the sun shines it will shine out the clearer.

Those were the stories that stayed with you.

That meant something.

Even if you were too small to understand why.

But I think, Mr. Frodo, I do understand.

I know now.

Folk in those stories had lots of chances of turning back only they didn't.

Because they were holding on to something.

Frodo : What are we holding on to, Sam?

Sam : That there's some good in this world, Mr. Frodo. And it's worth fighting for.

The Church is clear in the path she lays out this Lenten season: Christ, the light, the teller and the subject of the Greatest Story Ever Told, is leading us on this journey. Our task is to keep burning bright for each other. We need not to despair, but to trust in the Lord who desires to untie us and let us go free.

Solemnity of the Annunciation

Today, on the Solemnity of the Annunciation, we celebrate one of the most decisive moments in the history of salvation — the moment when the eternal Word took flesh in the womb of the Virgin Mary. It is a mystery so profound that the Church returns to it again and again in her liturgy — and perhaps some of you have noticed: this is the third time this year we have heard this very Gospel. It was proclaimed on the Solemnity of the Immaculate Conception, again on the Feast of Our Lady of Guadalupe, and now today, on March 25th, the day when eternity entered into time.

We return to this Gospel so often because it unveils the mystery of our faith: God becomes man, not by force, but by the free, humble, and generous "yes" of a young woman in Nazareth. This "yes" is the heart of today's celebration, and it is beautifully expressed in an Italian word: *disponibilità* — a word that means *availability, readiness*, or *willingness* — but also something more. It means making oneself completely open and receptive to the will of another. Today we contemplate Mary's *disponibilità* — her total openness to the will of God — and we ask how we can imitate this in our own lives.

In today's Gospel from Luke 1:26–38, the Angel Gabriel appears to Mary with the most astonishing announcement ever made: "You will conceive in your womb and bear a son, and you shall name him Jesus."

But the hinge of the entire narrative — indeed, of the entire history of redemption — rests on Mary's response: *"Behold, I am the handmaid of the Lord. Let it be done to me according to your word."*

This is Mary's *disponibilità* — not simply submission, but active and joyful openness to God's plan. She doesn't fully understand what will happen. She is "greatly troubled." But she trusts, she listens, and she responds with faith.

Saint Bernard of Clairvaux, in one of his most famous homilies, imagines the whole world holding its breath, waiting for Mary's answer:

"You have heard, O Virgin, that you will conceive and bear a son; you have heard that it will not be by man but by the Holy Spirit. The angel awaits an answer; it is time for him to return to God who sent him. We too are waiting, O Lady, for your word of compassion; the sentence of condemnation weighs heavily upon us. The price of our salvation is offered to you. We shall be set free at once if you consent. Tearful Adam with his sorrowing family begs this of you, O loving Virgin, in their exile from Paradise. Abraham begs it, David begs it. The whole world begs it. Answer quickly, O Virgin! Speak the word which earth and heaven are waiting to hear. Behold, the desired of all nations is at your door." — *Homily IV: In Praise of the Virgin Mother*, §8–9 (*PL* 183:70–71).

And with her fiat — her "Let it be" — the Word becomes flesh.

The early Church Fathers saw in Mary the New Eve, whose obedience unties the knot of Eve's disobedience. Saint Irenaeus writes: "And thus also it was that the knot of Eve's disobedience was loosed by the obedience of Mary. For what the virgin Eve had bound fast through unbelief, this did the Virgin Mary set free through faith."— *Adversus Haereses*, III.22.4.

Mary's *disponibilità* is the model of Christian discipleship — a heart open to grace and ready to respond in faith.

Saint Thomas Aquinas, in his *Summa Theologiae* (ST III, q. 30), emphasizes the dignity and necessity of Mary's consent. God could have acted without her, but He chose to respect her freedom: *"The Annunciation was fittingly made to the Blessed Virgin before she conceived the Word incarnate, because this was becoming to the dignity of both Mother and Son — that she might become a mother not without the use of reason, but with full consent."*

In other words, Mary is not a passive instrument, but a fully engaged partner in God's saving plan — an exemplar of how grace perfects nature without violating freedom.

The Second Reading from Hebrews 10 reveals that Mary's *disponibilità* is not her own invention — it mirrors the very *disponibilità* of her Son: *"Sacrifice and offering you did not desire, but a body you prepared for me... Then I said, 'Behold, I come to do your will, O God.'"*

Christ's entire mission is one of self-giving obedience — of radical availability to the Father's will. What Mary says in Nazareth, Christ will say again in Gethsemane: *"Not my will, but yours be done."*

And this, dear friends, is not just the path for Mary or for Christ — it is the path for every Christian. *Disponibilità* is not something reserved for mystics or visionaries. It is the daily openness to God's will, in the ordinary duties of our vocations, in the interruptions we didn't plan, in the sufferings we didn't choose.

The first reading from Isaiah reminds us that God's plan always begins with a promise: *"The virgin shall conceive and bear a son, and shall name him Emmanuel."* God always initiates; we are invited to respond.

Disponibilità is how we live out Psalm 40, the responsorial for today: *"Here I am, Lord; I come to do your will."*

In Lent, as we draw closer to the mysteries of the Passion, we are reminded that true holiness is not doing great things for God, but letting Him do great things through us. *Disponibilità* is not about heroics; it is about *surrender* — and trust.

So how can we live Mary's *disponibilità*? May I suggest the following? By daily prayer, where we listen like she did. By acts of service, offered without complaint. By saying yes to what God asks of us — even when we don't understand it fully. By letting our own "fiat" echo hers: *"Let it be done to me according to your word."*

Today, on this third hearing of the Annunciation Gospel this liturgical year, the Church invites us to stop, reflect, and respond more deeply. Mary's *disponibilità* is not just a historical event — it is a pattern for our lives.

Let us ask her — Our Lady of the Fiat — to teach us how to be truly available to God: open, trusting, obedient, and joyful. O Mary, cause of our joy and model of our hope, help us to say with you: *Ecce ancilla Domini — fiat mihi secundum verbum tuum.*

Solemnity of Saint Patrick

There is a book which was published in 1995 entitled *How the Irish Saved Civilization* by Thomas Cahill. It is very true that the Irish did indeed save civilization. They went from a barbaric tribe, one which even the mighty Roman Empire could not conquer, to the ones who became, in many ways, the guiding light for both culture and Church, throughout Europe, and indeed, throughout America.

Where I come from, there is a friendly rivalry between Irish-Americans and Italian-Americans, and, growing up, one of my teachers in grade school tried to convince her class of sixth graders that Saint Patrick was really Italian. Even as a young boy, I wasn't buying it! He may have been a Roman Briton, but he was not Italian! (I say this jokingly as a priest who is assigned to Rome, Italy, and as someone who has ministered in Italian-American parishes in my Diocese!) We do know that Patrick was not Irish. At least not by birth!

Patrick comes to Ireland and makes these wild women and men Christian, and boy, does he do a good job. Cahill, in his book, comments: "In becoming an Irishman, Patrick wedded his world to theirs, his faith to their life…Patrick found a way of swimming down to the depths of the Irish psyche and warming and transforming Irish imagination – making it more humane and more noble while keeping it Irish."

What does it mean to be Irish? Sigmund Freud stated: "This is one race of people for whom psychoanalysis is of no use whatsoever."

Richard Sandhurst, an Englishman, stated: ""*The [Irish] people are thus inclined: religious, frank, amorous, ireful, sufferable of infinite pains, vain-glorious, with many sorcerers, excellent horsemen,*

delighted with warring, great almes-givers and surpassing in hospital-
ity. The lewder sort (both clerics and lay people alike) are sensual and
loose in living. They are sharp-witted, lovers of learning, adventurous,
kind-hearted and secret in displeasure."

So, what are some Irish tendencies? Without falling into stereo-
types and generalities, to be Irish means to feel deeply and to believe
dramatically. It means to think you are cool and collected, that you
are tough and unflappable, but, in reality, you wear your heart on
your sleeve, and, when you believe, you really, really believe. The
Irish are a Catholic people; it's ingrained into the culture and no-
where is this more apparent than in the contemporary conflict between a secular Ireland and a traditionally Catholic Ireland.

The contribution of the Irish to the Church is immense. In fact,
the truth of the matter is that we would not have individual confession if not for the Irish. And this is not even to mention the fact that
the U.S. Roman Catholic Church is, in fact, very Irish historically.
The model of diocesan and parochial life from the Northeast historically was the model, and, by and large, it is this model that was the
basis of parish life in the United States for the greater part of the
20th Century.

And the contribution of the Irish to the world was immense. Listen to Cahill's description:

Wherever they went the Irish brought with them their books,
many unseen in Europe for centuries and tied to their waists as signs
of triumph, just as Irish heroes had once tied to their waists their
enemies' heads. Where they went they brought their love of learning
and their skills in bookmaking. In the bays and valleys of their exile,
they reestablished literacy and breathed new life into the exhausted

literary culture of Europe. And that is how the Irish saved civilization.

Love of learning, love of books, this is a very Irish contribution to our world!

Although I have spent a great number of the years of my life downplaying the "Irishness" of my heritage, as I get older, I recognize that I am very Irish-American. I grew up, at the time, in a very Irish area of New York. Almost every kid I knew growing up was Irish-American. I recognize the fact that in many ways, I have what some would call a very Irish temperament- a bit of the melancholy, a love of the storytelling, and the tendency to hyperbole of the Irish. Describing the Irish temperament, Cahill writes: "They pursued the wondrous deed, the heroic gesture: fighting...drinking, art - poetry for intense emotion..." I pray that I use that intense emotion for my prayer life, my preaching, my celebration of the Mass, and in my studies, teaching, and writing. And yet, there are snakes present in me that need to be driven out. Perhaps you have them too, even if you do not have Irish heritage.

Patrick drove out the snakes from Ireland. He was driving out the snakes of sin, of falsehood, of hypocrisy. I need the prayers of Patrick and the grace and power of Jesus to drive out those snakes, that *pusilla anima*, that fearful soul, that soul that cares more for the things of this world which is passing away instead of focusing in on what truly matters- the Lord and the things of the Lord! Jesus, Our Lord, worked through this emotional, loving, sentimental, pugnacious people, these Irish, who never could be conquered by the Romans, by the British, and, I believe, cannot be conquered even by secularism and anti-Catholicism today. Drive those snakes out of all of us, those snakes of sin and selfishness, those snakes of secularity and sensuality, Patrick, and through the intercession of all the Saints, Blesseds, and Venerables of Ireland, and through the Eucharist we share, bring us to a Blessed Easter.

Solemnity of Saint Joseph

Today, the Church celebrates with solemn joy Saint Joseph, Spouse of the Blessed Virgin Mary and Guardian of the Redeemer — a man of profound silence, steadfast action, and extraordinary holiness. While the Gospels give us not a single word from his lips, the Fathers of the Church saw in Saint Joseph a man of immense spiritual stature, entrusted with the earthly guardianship of the Son of God.

Saint Joseph stands at the very heart of salvation history, not by preaching or performing miracles, but by his obedience, humility, and contemplative strength. Today, we allow the early Fathers of the Church to guide our meditation, helping us see in Joseph a mirror of divine fatherhood and a model of Christian discipleship.

The Gospel of Matthew calls Joseph a "just man" (Matthew 1:19), and the Fathers of the Church never tired of reflecting on what that means. According to Origen, *"Joseph was not only just in the sense of being virtuous, but he was also wise and prudent, discerning in the face of mystery, able to act without sin and without shame."* (*Homilies on the Gospel of Matthew*)

Joseph's justice, then, was not mere adherence to the Law — it was an openness to the movement of God's Spirit, even when God's plan was veiled in mystery.

When he learned that Mary was with child, Joseph resolved to divorce her quietly. He did not act in anger or haste. The Fathers emphasize that he was unwilling to expose her, not because he doubted her virtue, but because he recognized the presence of something divine and mysterious beyond his comprehension.

St. Jerome, in his commentary on Matthew, writes: *"Joseph knew Mary's holiness and feared to dwell with such sanctity. He believed more in mystery than in sin."* This humility — this holy fear of God's mystery — is what makes Joseph great.

The Gospel of Luke shows us Joseph as the guardian of Jesus and Mary, quietly and faithfully fulfilling his role in the hidden life of Nazareth. Though we often associate Mary with the title *Theotokos* — "God-bearer" — the Fathers recognized that Joseph too bore a title of sacred responsibility: *custos Redemptoris* — guardian of the Redeemer. St. John Chrysostom writes: *"God chose Joseph to be the protector of Mary and Jesus because he had the virtues necessary to guard the ones who were most dear to God Himself."*

In Joseph, the Word made flesh finds shelter. In Joseph, Mary finds a strong and faithful spouse. And in Joseph, we are given a model of fatherhood, chastity, obedience, and perseverance in the hidden life.

Our first reading from 2 Samuel 7 reminds us of God's covenant with David: *"I will raise up your heir... and I will establish his kingdom forever."*

Though Joseph is not the biological father of Jesus, he is Son of David, and thus he becomes the link between the promises made to David and their fulfillment in Christ. The Gospel does not refer to Jesus as "the son of Mary and Joseph" out of error but to show that Joseph's paternal role is real and essential in the divine plan.

In Joseph, we see the Church's calling: to guard the mysteries of God with faith, reverence, and devotion. Just as Joseph protected and nourished the Body of Christ in the Incarnation, the Church is called to protect and nourish the Body of Christ in the Eucharist, in the poor, in her mission, and in the domestic church of the family. In a world obsessed with noise, image, and assertion, Joseph offers the counter-witness of silence, integrity, and interiority.

The Solemnity of Saint Joseph invites us to entrust our lives to his intercession, just as Jesus and Mary entrusted theirs to his care.

Whether you are a father, a husband, a worker, a religious, or a young person discerning God's call, Saint Joseph stands before you as a companion and guide. He does not speak — but he listens. He does not preach — but he obeys. He does not boast — but he serves.

Let us heed the words that the Church has repeated for centuries: *Ite ad Ioseph — Go to Joseph.* He will lead us to Mary. And Mary will always lead us to Jesus.

Saint Joseph, guardian of the Redeemer and pillar of the Church, pray for us.

Palm Sunday of the Lord's Passion

Interestingly enough, the rubrics for the Mass of this Palm Sunday of the Lord's Passion, state the following: "After the narrative of the Passion, a brief homily should take place, if appropriate. A period of silence may also be observed."

On the one Sunday of the entire liturgical year in which we read of the passion and death of our Lord Jesus, why would the Church, in her wisdom, suggest that "a brief homily" should take place? Why would Mother Church suggest that perhaps even silence might be more appropriate than a homily?

I believe because we should let these events of the Passion and Death, so dolorous, yet so glorious speak for themselves. We should just listen to this story, one we have heard for many years, and just experience it.

On a day like Palm Sunday of the Lord's Passion, maybe all the words, all the explanations we can give, perhaps it will just get in the way. For this Sunday, my advice is that all of us should just listen to the story, as if we're hearing it for the first time. Listen to this fierce little human drama, all happening on the natural level. Listen to how fallen humanity's sin, its greed, its jealousy, its hypocrisy, put to death He who is life. Listen to how the All Beautiful One is scarred, broken, bloodied, beaten, bruised for our offenses. Listen to how the Innocent One bears the weight of our guilt.

Look for how everything in this Gospel that is taking place on the human level is also taking place at the very same time on the supernatural level. As Pilate and Herod have their day on earth, from the underworld, does Satan.

Listen to this story with open, attentive, and loving ears, fully conscious and fully aware of all that is happening and perceive it for what it is: the greatest love story told. He who is love, Jesus, He who is mercy, opens his arms wide on the cross in an embrace of love for you and me and, in His suffering, we share in that victory. Listen in the silence.

Evening Mass of the Lord's Supper

Tonight, we stand at the threshold of the Sacred Triduum—the holiest days of the Church's year—beginning with the Evening Mass of the Lord's Supper. Saint John tells us that Jesus, "having loved His own who were in the world, loved them to the end" (Jn 13:1). These words are more than narrative. They are the interpretive key to everything that unfolds in these sacred hours.

This evening, we contemplate the mysteries that lie at the very heart of our faith: the institution of the Holy Eucharist, the institution of the ministerial priesthood, and the Lord's commandment of charity expressed in the washing of feet. Beneath all three runs one unifying current—the mystery of *kenosis*, the self-emptying love of God poured out in Christ, who gives everything to the Father and to us.

Saint Paul, in his Letter to the Philippians, reveals the inner movement of this mystery: "Though He was in the form of God, He did not count equality with God a thing to be grasped, but emptied Himself" (*ekenōsen*) (Phil 2:6–7). This divine self-emptying—this *kenosis*—becomes visible on this night. It is seen when the Master bends to wash the feet of His disciples: God kneeling before man. It is seen in the breaking of bread and the pouring of wine: God giving His very Body and Blood as food and drink. It is seen in the silence of Gethsemane, where He prays in agony, "Not My will, but Yours be done."

The Eucharist is not a mere remembrance nor a symbolic gesture. It is the living act of God's total gift. In this sacrament, the Son gives Himself without remainder. He offers not something, but Himself—

Body, Blood, Soul, and Divinity—so that we might share in His divine life. To receive Him is to be drawn into the form of His surrender.

The Fathers of the Church saw in this night the culmination of divine pedagogy—the moment when the shadows of the Old Covenant are transformed into the radiant light of fulfillment. Saint Augustine exhorted his hearers: "Recognize in the bread what hung on the Cross; recognize in the chalice what flowed from His side" (*Sermon 272*). Saint Cyril of Jerusalem likewise urged: "Do not regard the Eucharistic elements as ordinary bread and wine. They are the Body and Blood of Christ, as He declared... Taste and see that the Lord is good" (*Mystagogical Catecheses*, 4).

Yet what is most striking in John's Gospel is not a recounting of the words of institution, but the humble gesture of the Lord rising from supper, removing His outer garment, and washing the feet of His disciples. Here the Eucharist becomes visible in action. The Word-made-flesh stoops low, and the Bread of Life becomes the Servant of life. The Eucharist is not only to be received—it is to be lived.

This night is also the beginning of the ministerial priesthood. When Christ says, "Do this in memory of Me," He entrusts to His apostles a share in His own self-giving love. The priest is not simply one who presides at sacred rites, but one configured to the Eucharistic Christ—broken in order to feed others, poured out in obedience to the Father, living not for himself but for his people. Yet every baptized Christian, too, is invited into this priestly pattern of life, this Eucharistic service made manifest in humble love.

We do not gather tonight merely to remember something that happened two thousand years ago. In the sacred liturgy, the mystery becomes present. The Upper Room becomes our sanctuary; the Passover becomes our sacrifice; the Bread of Life is once again placed into our hands. But this gift is not given only for adoration—it is given for transformation. We are called to become what we receive, to be a Eucharistic people who live the *kenosis* of Christ in the ordinary and hidden places of life: in patience with the difficult, in service to the poor, in forgiving what seems unforgivable, in saying with Mary, "Let it be done unto me," and with Jesus, "This is my Body, given for you."

Let us, then, enter this holy night with reverence and love. Let us kneel before the God who kneels before us. Let us receive the Bread of Life with hearts open to be changed. And let us learn from Him what it means to pour ourselves out in love, so that in the mystery of the Cross and Resurrection we too may be filled with divine life.

"For having loved His own who were in the world, He loved them to the end" (Jn 13:1).

May we, who receive His Body and Blood tonight, learn to love in the same way.

Good Friday

"Behold the man."

With these words—*Ecce Homo*—Pontius Pilate speaks more truth than he knows. Before him stands Jesus: beaten, mocked, crowned with thorns. A man disfigured beyond recognition. A man who is God. A God who suffers.

Today we do not come to celebrate.

We come to behold.

To watch.

To kneel.

To weep.

To adore.

This day is not a reenactment. It is not sacred theater. We do not merely recall the Passion — we enter it. The Church stands at Calvary. We stand with Mary, the Mother of Sorrows, at the foot of the Cross. We listen once more to the Word made flesh, now silent, "like a lamb led to the slaughter" (Isa 53:7). The prophet foresaw it: "He was spurned and avoided by men, a man of suffering... pierced for our offenses, crushed for our sins" (Isa 53:3, 5).

This is the Suffering Servant who bears the weight of sin — and yet opens not His mouth. The scandal lies in this: He is innocent. More than innocent — He is holy. He is the eternal Son of God, without stain or shadow, and yet He chooses the path of suffering. Why? Because, Isaiah says, "By His wounds, we were healed." This is not only a story of suffering; it is a story of substitution. He takes our place. The wrath that justice demands falls on Him. And the Son says, "Yes, Father. Let it be done."

The Cross is not merely a moral example. It is the mystery of *kenosis* — the self-emptying of the eternal Son who descends into the very depths of human rejection, into the farthest reach of the creature's "no" to God. Here, love empties itself completely. God goes to the lowest place so that no one might remain there.

This is not passive endurance. It is active, creative love — divine love taking on the weakness of the flesh and transforming suffering from within. The Letter to the Hebrews reminds us that we do not have a high priest who is unable to sympathize with our weakness, but one who has been tested in every way, yet without sin. In the Old Covenant, the high priest stood apart from the victim. In the New Covenant, the High Priest becomes the victim. The altar is the Cross. The priest is Christ. The offering is His own flesh.

That is why in John's Gospel there is no cry of abandonment. There is, instead, a sovereign peace. "It is finished." The Lord is not overcome by death — He offers Himself to it. "No one takes my life from me," He says; "I lay it down of my own accord" (Jn 10:18). What appears as defeat is in truth His enthronement. The inscription above the Cross — *Jesus of Nazareth, King of the Jews* — is no irony. It is proclamation. The Cross is His throne; His power is the power of love; His crown is made of thorns.

Tonight, the altar is stripped, the tabernacle empty, the sanctuary bare. There is no Mass. Yet the silence is not absence — it is presence in another key. It is the silence of a love that has poured itself out completely. The Word has spoken His final word: "It is finished."

Let those words echo in your heart.

It is finished — your guilt.

It is finished — your shame.

It is finished — the dominion of sin and death.

Saint Augustine once said that the Cross is "the pulpit from which Christ preached His love to the world." And we are His listeners. We stand beside Mary and John. We stay. We remain. We love. We venerate the Cross not as ornament but as the Tree of Life, the wood by which Adam's curse is undone.

From His pierced side flow blood and water — the sacraments of the Church. As Eve was formed from Adam's side, so the Church is born from Christ's. This is the new creation: the world remade in the crucified love of God.

And so we kneel. We kiss the Cross. We adore — not defeat, but victory through surrender. The body will be laid in the tomb; the stone will be rolled before the entrance; and silence will fall upon the earth. Yet it is not the silence of despair — it is the stillness before dawn.

The ancient Fathers say that Christ descends into hell — not to be held, but to shatter its gates. Love reaches even there.

So we come. We kneel. We behold the Man. We embrace the Cross. We love. And we wait.

Because the tomb is not the final word.

Love will rise.

Easter Vigil

"This is the day the Lord has made; let us rejoice and be glad."

Christ is risen! He is truly risen! Alleluia!

Tonight, the Church stands in the radiant stillness between death and life, between darkness and light, between the Cross and the empty tomb. The fire is kindled, the Word proclaimed, and the cry of Alleluia returns to our lips. We do not gather tonight to recall a myth or a memory, but to behold a reality that has broken into history: the tomb is empty; the stone is rolled away; the Crucified One is alive.

The Resurrection of Jesus Christ is not the conclusion of the Gospel—it is the beginning of a new creation. The light that bursts forth from the tomb is the same light that shone at the dawn of time, now transfigured and made eternal. Easter is not an ending—it is an explosion that reverberates through the cosmos and into the hearts of those who believe.

The Vigil begins, fittingly, in darkness, where the Word of God first spoke creation into being. In Genesis, we hear that "God said, 'Let there be light,' and there was light." That first light shattered the chaos of the void. Tonight, that same Word, now made flesh, speaks once more: "Let there be light"—and the darkness of sin and death is dispelled forever.

Saint Thomas Aquinas reminds us that *the work of creation and the work of redemption flow from the same divine goodness.* The first creation brought forth life from nothing; the new creation brings forth life from death. In the beginning, God breathed into Adam the breath of life; tonight, the Risen Christ breathes the Spirit of new life into His Church.

The story continues through Abraham and Isaac, through Moses and the crossing of the Red Sea, through the prophets and psalmists—all leading to this night. The Exodus, that mighty deliverance from Egypt, prefigures baptism: as Israel passed through the waters from slavery to freedom, so we pass through the waters of the font from death to life. The Paschal Candle, burning before us, is the pillar of fire that guides us through the darkness into the land of promise.

In the first reading of the Mass, from the Acts of the Apostles, Saint Peter stands before the Gentiles and proclaims: "They put Him to death by hanging Him on a tree; this man God raised on the third day." Here we hear the heart of the apostolic preaching—the *kerygma* itself. The Resurrection is not a private consolation or a poetic symbol; it is the defining fact of history.

And Peter—the one who denied Christ three times—is the first to preach His victory. The coward becomes the cornerstone of faith. Grace transforms weakness into witness. The Resurrection is not only the vindication of Jesus; it is the restoration of all who failed Him. The Risen Lord does not return in vengeance but in mercy, saying, "Peace be with you."

To believe in the Resurrection is to be sent. Easter joy is missionary by nature. As Peter was commissioned to preach, so we are sent into a weary world to proclaim that death does not have the final word.

Saint Paul tells us in the letter to the Colossians, "If you have been raised with Christ, seek what is above." This is not a call to escapism or mere sentimentality—it is the moral and mystical consequence of the Resurrection.

We have died with Christ in baptism, and now we live no longer for ourselves but for Him. The old leaven of sin is gone; the new dough of grace is rising within us. The Resurrection calls us to set our minds on heavenly things, not to abandon the world, but to see it in the light of eternity.

As Aquinas teaches, *grace perfects nature*—it does not destroy it. The life of the Risen Christ does not abolish our humanity; it fulfills it. The resurrection life is not future only; it begins now, wherever mercy is shown, truth is spoken, and love triumphs over fear.

Then we come to the Gospel—the first light of Easter morning. Mary Magdalene comes to the tomb while it is still dark. The darkness of sin and grief still lingers, but dawn is near. She finds the stone rolled away, and runs to tell Peter and John. The two apostles race to the tomb; John, the beloved disciple, arrives first, and when he enters, he sees and believes.

What does he see? Empty cloths. What does he believe? That the promises of Jesus are true—that death has been conquered, and love has won.

Saint Thomas Aquinas, in his *Commentary on John*, says that the Resurrection is not one miracle among others, but the miracle that confirms all others: *"If Christ had not risen, the world would have remained in darkness; but in His Resurrection, the whole universe is illumined."* (*In Ioannem*, c. 20). The beloved disciple is the first to see this light and believe; through his eyes, the Church begins to see.

The Fathers of the Church saw Easter as the dawn of a new creation. Saint Gregory of Nyssa called the Resurrection "the re-creation of the human race." Saint Irenaeus taught that as Adam's disobedience brought death, so Christ, the new Adam, restores life. And Saint Augustine proclaimed, "The Lord's Resurrection is our hope, just as His Cross is our ransom... The tomb becomes a womb; the place of death becomes the birthplace of eternity."

What began in a garden with Adam begins again in a garden with Christ. The first Adam hid among the trees; the second Adam is raised among the tombs. The stone rolled away is not merely a sign of absence; it is the visible symbol that the wall between humanity and God has been forever removed.

What does Easter demand of us? Not only belief, but transformation. Not only wonder, but witness. Not only joy, but mission.

Like Mary Magdalene, we must run to announce the good news. Like Peter, we must proclaim Christ crucified and risen. Like John, we must see and believe.

In a world gripped by fear, the Resurrection makes us people of hope.

In a culture obsessed with death, we live as witnesses to life.

In a society deafened by noise, we carry the stillness of the empty tomb, where God acts beyond all human expectation.

Tonight, we do not simply remember a past event—we step into its reality. The same Risen Lord who walked out of the tomb now stands among us. His light shines in the darkness, and the darkness cannot overcome it.

"This is the day the Lord has made; let us rejoice and be glad." (Ps 118:24)

This is the day when creation begins anew.

This is the day when sin is forgiven and death defeated.

This is the day when love proves stronger than the grave.

Let us live, then, as Easter people—transfigured by grace, radiant with joy, and steadfast in hope. For Christ is risen! He is truly risen! Alleluia.

Easter Sunday

Christ is risen! He is truly risen! Alleluia!

Today, the Church does not simply retell an old story — she announces a reality that has shattered history. The stone is rolled away. The tomb is empty. The Crucified One is alive. Easter is not the conclusion of the Gospel but its beginning — the dawn of a new creation. The light that bursts from the tomb radiates through every age, illuminating hearts darkened by fear and death.

In the Gospel of John, Mary Magdalene comes to the tomb while it is still dark. She finds the stone rolled away and runs to Peter and John. They come, they see, and the beloved disciple *"saw and believed"* (Jn 20:8).

What did he believe? Not merely that the body was missing, but that everything Jesus had promised was true — that He would suffer, die, and rise on the third day. At the empty tomb, faith begins to see with the eyes of love; revelation breaks through the night.

Saint Thomas Aquinas teaches that the Resurrection is not one miracle among others but the foundation of all faith: *"If Christ had not risen, our preaching would be in vain."* (*Summa Theologiae* III, q. 53, a. 3; cf. 1 Cor 15:14)

And elsewhere he writes the principle that grounds all theology: "Grace does not destroy nature but perfects it." (*Summa Theologiae* I, q. 1, a. 8)

The Risen Christ does not erase our humanity — He restores and elevates it. The wounds remain, but now they shine.

In Acts 10, Peter proclaims: *"They put Him to death by hanging Him on a tree, but God raised Him on the third day and granted that*

He be visible... to us who ate and drank with Him after He rose from the dead."

The Resurrection immediately sends forth a mission. It is not a private consolation but a public proclamation. And the one who preaches is Peter — the same man who denied the Lord. Now forgiven and transformed, he becomes the first witness of Easter faith. Grace turns weakness into strength and failure into fidelity.

Saint John Chrysostom, in his famous Easter homily, declares: *"Hell took a body, and met God face to face. It took earth, and encountered heaven. It took what it saw, and was overcome by what it did not see."* (*Paschal Homily*, PG 59:723)

The Cross, once the instrument of death, has become the throne of life. The victory of Easter is not the reversal of Good Friday but its revelation. Love has triumphed in weakness.

Saint Paul writes: *"If you have been raised with Christ, seek the things that are above, where Christ is seated at the right hand of God."* (Col 3:1)

This is no abstraction. Through baptism we have died with Christ and risen with Him. The same power that raised Jesus from the tomb now works in us. Easter is not only what happened to Christ — it is what happens in the believer who lives by grace.

As Paul says again, *"Cleanse out the old leaven, that you may be a new lump, as you really are unleavened. For Christ, our Pasch, has been sacrificed."* (1 Cor 5:7)

We are invited to live no longer under the shadow of sin but in the light of divine charity — to become new bread for the world.

The early Fathers saw Easter as the beginning of a new creation.

Saint Gregory of Nyssa speaks of the Resurrection as *"the re-creation of our nature."* (*Oratio Catechetica Magna*, 32)

Saint Irenaeus writes: *"As by one man's disobedience death entered in, so by one man's obedience life is restored to the human race."*(*Adversus Haereses*, III.18.7)

And Saint Augustine proclaims *"The Lord's Resurrection is our hope; the Lord's Passion is our redemption."* (*Sermon 229N, 1*)

The tomb, Augustine says elsewhere, becomes a womb — the place of death becomes the birthplace of eternity. What began in a garden with Adam begins again in a garden with Christ. The stone rolled away is the sign that the barrier between God and humanity has been removed forever.

What then does Easter demand of us?

It calls not only for belief but for transformation; not only for joy but for mission. Like Mary Magdalene, we must run to tell others what we have seen. Like Peter, we must proclaim boldly that Christ is Lord. Like John, we must see and believe even amid mystery.

In a world gripped by fear, Easter makes us people of hope. In a culture shadowed by death, it makes us witnesses to life. In a society filled with noise, it makes us bearers of the silence of the empty tomb — the silence where God has acted beyond all expectation.

Tonight, we do not merely recall a past event. We enter its living power. The Risen One is here. His light shines in the darkness, and the darkness has not overcome it.

"This is the day the Lord has made; let us rejoice and be glad." (Ps 118:24)

This is the day when creation is renewed, when sin is conquered, and death defeated. This is the day when love proves stronger than the grave.

Let us live as Easter people — transfigured by grace, radiant with joy, and steadfast in hope.

Christ is risen! He is truly risen! Alleluia!

Divine Mercy Sunday

On this Second Sunday of Easter, the Church turns our eyes to the Risen Christ, whose first words to His fearful apostles are simple and divine: *"Peace be with you."*

He does not begin with reproach. He does not chastise Peter for his denial, nor the others for their flight. He enters the locked room and speaks *shalom* — that deep biblical peace that restores what sin has broken, reconciles what was estranged, and binds together what was shattered.

Saint Augustine defines peace not merely as the absence of conflict but as *"tranquillitas ordinis"* — "the tranquility of order." (*De Civitate Dei*, XIX, 13). True peace, he teaches, is the harmony that arises when all things are rightly ordered under God, when love reigns and justice is fulfilled.

The apostles are not yet at peace. They are behind locked doors, imprisoned by fear and shame. Yet the peace Christ brings is not an emotion — it is a gift. It flows from His victory over sin and death. Saint Thomas Aquinas, following Augustine, writes that *"peace is the work of justice, and the effect of charity."* (*Summa Theologiae* II-II, q. 29, a. 3, ad 1). For Aquinas, peace is not passive stillness but the ordered calm of a soul united to God in love. Because Christ, through His Passion and Resurrection, has restored the right order between humanity and God, He alone can truly say: *"Peace be with you."*

When Jesus speaks peace, He immediately shows them His wounds. The Risen Christ does not conceal the marks of His Passion. His glorified body still bears the nails and the spear — not as scars of failure, but as luminous signs of love. These wounds are the fountains of mercy, the visible tokens of invisible grace. As the prophet Isaiah foretold, *"By His wounds we are healed"* (Is 53:5).

The same hands once pierced now confer the Spirit and the power to forgive. *"As the Father has sent Me, so I send you... Receive the Holy Spirit. Whose sins you forgive are forgiven them."* (Jn 20:21-23). The peace of Christ overflows immediately into mission; the mercy He gives becomes the mercy we must offer.

On this Divine Mercy Sunday, the Church rejoices in this living image of compassion. The Risen Lord does not wait for our perfection — He steps into fear with forgiveness, into shame with peace. His mercy is not sentiment but substance, the very life of God poured into wounded humanity.

Then there is Thomas. Absent when the Lord first appears, he refuses to believe without seeing. Yet when Jesus comes again, He meets Thomas not with anger, but invitation: *"Put your finger here and see My hands; and bring your hand and put it into My side. Do not be unbelieving, but believe."* (Jn 20:27).

Thomas touches love incarnate, and faith bursts forth from his lips: *"My Lord and my God!"* (Jn 20:28). This is not mere recognition of Jesus' survival; it is the highest confession of faith in all the Gospels — a declaration of divinity. In those wounds, Thomas sees the mercy of God Himself. Saint Thomas Aquinas later echoes this moment in his Eucharistic hymn *Adoro te devote*: *"Though I do not see Your wounds as Thomas did, I confess You to be my God."* (*Adoro te devote*, v. 2)

The same faith that transformed Thomas is offered to us at every Mass, where the Risen Lord again stands before His Church, saying, *"Peace be with you."*

Saint Peter, in today's second reading, reminds us that faith opens into joy: *"Although you have not seen Him, you love Him; and even though you do not see Him now, you believe in Him and rejoice with an indescribable and glorious joy, as you attain the goal of your faith — the salvation of your souls."* (1 Pt 1:8-9)

That is the call of Easter: to live in peace, to be shaped by mercy, and to radiate joy. The peace of Christ is not withdrawal from the world, but transformation within it. The wounds of Christ are not erased from history; they become the channels through which grace enters it.

Dear brothers and sisters, the Risen Christ still stands among us and speaks the same word: *"Peace be with you."* Let His peace dwell in your hearts. Let His wounds be your strength. Let His mercy be your mission.

And let the confession of Thomas be our own: *"My Lord and my God."*

May we go forth as Easter people — not only to believe in peace but to live it, not only to receive mercy but to show it, not only to rejoice in the Resurrection but to embody it.

Christ is risen! He is truly risen! Alleluia!

Third Sunday of Easter

On this Third Sunday of Easter, the Church places before us one of the most beautiful and mysterious encounters in all of Scripture — the story of the disciples on the road to Emmaus. It is a story of sorrow turned to joy, of blindness turned to sight, of despair transfigured into hope. It is not only their story; it is our own.

Every Eucharist is an Emmaus road. Every believer is called to this same journey — from confusion to clarity, from discouragement to faith, from absence to presence.

The two disciples are walking away from Jerusalem — away from the place of the Passion, away from the empty tomb, away from the hope they had once carried. Their words echo with heartbreak: *"We were hoping that He would be the one to redeem Israel."* (Lk 24:21)

That phrase — *"We were hoping"* — is the sound of disappointment. It is the ache of every human heart that has felt God to be silent, or love to be lost, or meaning to have vanished.

Yet even as they walk away, Christ Himself draws near. The Risen Lord accompanies them in their confusion, though their eyes are "prevented from recognizing Him." (Lk 24:16). He does not begin with condemnation. He begins with presence.

Saint Augustine reflects on this mystery with exquisite simplicity: *"They were walking with the Lord, and yet they did not recognize Him. He was with them, and yet they were blind. So too are we, when we forget that He is always walking beside us, even in our sorrow."* (*Sermon 235, On the Easter Season*, PL 38:1118)

Christ listens first. Then He speaks. *"What are you discussing as you walk along?"* (Lk 24:17). This is the tenderness of divine pedagogy — to draw the human heart out of itself, to awaken desire, to prepare it for revelation.

Then, beginning with Moses and all the prophets, *"He interpreted to them in all the Scriptures the things concerning Himself."* (Lk 24:27). The divine interpreter opens the Word of God, revealing that the path of the Messiah — suffering, death, and glory — is not failure but fulfillment. The Cross is not erased; it is explained.

Saint Thomas Aquinas, commenting on this passage in his *Catena Aurea*, observes: *"Christ begins not with miracles, but with the Word; for it is faith, born of hearing, that opens the eyes of the soul."* (*Catena Aurea in Lucam*, ch. 24, lect. 4)

The disciples' hearts begin to burn — not because their problems vanish, but because their minds are illumined by truth and their hearts inflamed by love.

When they reach Emmaus, they beg Him: *"Stay with us, for it is nearly evening."* (Lk 24:29). And at table, He takes bread, blesses it, breaks it, and gives it to them. *"Then their eyes were opened, and they recognized Him."* (Lk 24:31).

This is the Eucharistic climax — the same fourfold action as at the Last Supper: He took, blessed, broke, and gave. Recognition dawns at the breaking of the bread. What had been spoken in Word is now made visible in Sacrament.

The risen Christ is not a memory — He is present, alive, and given. At that moment He vanishes, not because He is gone, but because He remains in a new way: sacramentally, mystically, in the Eucharist of the Church.

Once they recognize Him, the disciples do not remain in Emmaus. *"They set out at once and returned to Jerusalem."* (Lk 24:33).

Their despair is replaced by mission. The road they once traveled in defeat becomes the road of proclamation. They return to the place they had fled, bearing the joyful witness: *"The Lord has truly been raised!"* (Lk 24:34).

This is the pattern of Christian life: Word, Sacrament, and Mission — or more simply, encounter, communion, and witness. The heart that has burned with the Word and been nourished by the Bread cannot remain still; it must go forth.

This Gospel is not only the story of two disciples — it is the form of every Eucharist and the rhythm of every believer's life. In the Liturgy of the Word, Christ opens the Scriptures and causes our hearts to burn. In the Liturgy of the Eucharist, He breaks the Bread and opens our eyes. And in the sending forth, He commands us to proclaim what we have seen and heard: *"Go, announce the Gospel of the Lord."*

How often have we walked in our own confusion, speaking of disappointments, failing to recognize the One who walks beside us? Yet Christ never ceases to draw near. He enters our sorrow not as stranger but as Savior. He sets our hearts ablaze with the fire of His truth, and He makes Himself known in the breaking of the Bread.

The miracle of Easter is this: that Christ walks with us even when we are walking the wrong way — and by love, not by force, He turns us around.

"Were not our hearts burning within us?" Let that question accompany us this week. Let us return often to the Word, to the Breaking of the Bread, to the quiet companionship of Christ in prayer. Let our hearts burn again with faith and love, that we too might rise, return, and proclaim:

"The Lord has truly been raised! Alleluia!"

Fourth Sunday of Easter

On this Fourth Sunday of Easter, traditionally called Good Shepherd Sunday, the Church turns our eyes toward one of the most tender and powerful self-revelations of Christ. He is the Shepherd who knows His sheep, calls them by name, and leads them to life. Yet today, in Saint John's Gospel, the image shifts slightly. Before we hear of the Shepherd's voice and His staff, we first hear of the gate.

"Amen, amen, I say to you, I am the gate for the sheep." (Jn 10:7)

It is a strange image at first — Christ is not only the Shepherd but also the Gate. He is both the one who guards the flock and the one through whom all must pass.

Saint Thomas Aquinas, commenting on this passage, writes: *"Christ is the door because through Him we go in to the knowledge of God; He is the way, and He is also the end."* (*In Ioannem*, c.10, lect.1)

The sheepfold, he explains, is the Church. The sheep are those who listen to His voice. And the Gate — the only Gate — is Christ Himself. There is no access to the Father, no entrance into divine life, except through Him who is both Shepherd and Door.

This image speaks not only of protection but of intimacy. The Good Shepherd knows His sheep personally, not as part of a faceless herd but as beloved individuals. He calls each by name.

Saint Gregory the Great, preaching on this Gospel, says beautifully: *"To call His own sheep by name is to know their lives and to love them with eternal love."* (*Homiliae in Evangelia*, XIV, 3; PL 76:1129)

Christ contrasts Himself with those who "climb in another way"— thieves and robbers who scatter the flock. These are not only false teachers but also interior temptations — the counterfeit voices that promise freedom yet lead to captivity, that promise abundance but deliver emptiness.

In the ancient Near East, shepherds would lie down across the opening of the sheepfold at night. Their bodies themselves became the gate. The flock could not enter or leave except by passing over the shepherd's own body. What a perfect foreshadowing of Christ! On the Cross, He becomes the Gate in the most literal sense: His body is broken open, His side pierced, that through Him humanity might enter into the life of God.

The second reading echoes this mystery: *"By His wounds you have been healed. For you were straying like sheep, but have now returned to the Shepherd and Guardian of your souls."* (1 Pt 2:24–25)

Here the image deepens. Christ is not only the Shepherd and the Gate — He is also the Lamb who was slain. The One who leads us has first gone before us. He descends into our lostness to bring us home. The Shepherd bears the scent of the sheep. He is the wounded Shepherd, the only one we can trust.

"I came that they may have life, and have it more abundantly." (Jn 10:10)

This abundant life is not simply existence or human flourishing. It is divine life — *zoē* — the life of grace, the participation in the very life of God that begins in Baptism and is renewed in every Eucharist.

Saint Augustine, in his *Tractates on the Gospel of John*, meditates on this passage and writes: *"He is life, who said, 'I am the life.' He is not the life that you see with your eyes, nor the life that ends in death, but the life that even in death gives life."* (*Tractatus in Ioannem*, 47, 2; PL 35:1728)

This is why the Shepherd's voice resounds across every age: not to command from afar, but to draw near and to give life. He calls us not into safety alone, but into communion.

In a world filled with competing voices — the noise of self-sufficiency, of fear, of false promise — the question becomes deeply personal: *Whose voice am I following?* Only one voice calls you by name. Only one leads you through the gate into freedom and joy.

To follow the Good Shepherd is not to escape suffering, but to discover meaning within it. His rod and His staff do not spare us from the valley of the shadow of death, but they make it traversable. To walk behind Him is to trust that no darkness is final, no wound beyond redemption, no loss beyond His reach.

He leads, not by domination, but by love. He governs, not by control, but by self-offering. The Shepherd with wounds is the Shepherd who saves.

Let us listen again to His voice. Let us enter again through the only Gate that leads to life. Let us follow the One who has laid down His life for us — not from fear, but from love.

Christ is the Shepherd who seeks us, the Gate who guards us, the Lamb who redeems us, and the Life who sustains us. *"The Lord is my Shepherd; there is nothing I shall want."* (Ps 23:1) May we follow Him faithfully, until we too dwell forever in the house of the Lord.

Christ is risen! He is truly risen! Alleluia.

Fifth Sunday of Easter

On this Fifth Sunday of Easter, the Church gives us a Gospel often heard at funerals — Christ's words at the Last Supper: *"Do not let your hearts be troubled."* But these are not words of farewell or death. They are words of promise, of revelation, and of mission. In the light of Easter, this passage is not about absence but about preparation — not about loss, but about the foundation of Christian hope.

The disciples are afraid. They sense that something terrible is coming. Jesus meets their fear not with explanation, but with self-revelation. He shows them who He is — not merely a teacher or a prophet, but the very way to the Father: *"I am the way, and the truth, and the life; no one comes to the Father except through Me."* (Jn 14:6)

Saint Augustine reflects on this verse with characteristic precision and warmth: *"It was not enough for Him to say, 'I am the way,' unless He also said, 'I am the life'; lest we despair of ever reaching the goal. Nor was it enough to say, 'I am the life,' unless He also said, 'I am the truth'; lest we wander from the path."* (*Tractatus in Ioannem*, 69, 2; PL 35:1823)

Jesus reveals Himself as the journey and the destination, the map and the home. He is not one way among many — He is *the* Way. He is not one insight among others — He is *the* Truth. And He is not one source of vitality — He is *Life itself*, the living God made visible.

Then Philip, representing every human longing, pleads: *"Lord, show us the Father, and that will be enough for us."* (Jn 14:8) It is the cry of the heart — to see God, to know His face. And Jesus answers with words that pierce the mystery: *"Whoever has seen Me has seen the Father."* (Jn 14:9)

This is no metaphor. It is revelation. The invisible God has shown His face in Christ. As the Catechism of the Catholic Church teaches:

"In many and various ways God spoke of old to our fathers by the prophets, but in these last days He has spoken to us by a Son... Christ, the Son of God made man, is the Father's one, perfect, and unsurpassable Word." (CCC §65, citing Heb 1:1–2)

Saint Thomas Aquinas deepens this insight: *"To see Christ is to see the Father, not by bodily vision, but because the Son is the perfect image of the Father's essence."* (*Summa Theologiae*, I, q.43, a.5, ad 2)

To know Jesus, then, is not simply to learn about God — it is to enter into communion with God. In Christ, knowledge becomes relationship; vision becomes union.

Saint Peter, in the second reading, extends this mystery to us: *"Like living stones, let yourselves be built into a spiritual house."* (1 Pt 2:5)

Faith is not a private belief; it is incorporation into the living Body of Christ. We are not merely followers imitating a Master from afar — we are members of His Body, built upon the cornerstone rejected by men but chosen and precious in the sight of God. (cf. 1 Pt 2:6)

This means that we share His mission. The Church, born from His pierced side, continues His works in the world. That is why Jesus can say: *"Whoever believes in Me will do the works that I do, and greater ones than these."* (Jn 14:12)

What could be greater than raising the dead or healing the blind? The answer lies not in magnitude, but in mystery: the Church, animated by the Holy Spirit, participates in Christ's redemptive mission — bringing souls into communion with the Father through faith and the sacraments.

In the first reading from the Acts of the Apostles, we witness the establishment of the diaconate — a visible sign that the Church must serve both Word and Table, both truth and charity. This is not mere organization. It is the unfolding of divine order: a sacramental structure in which every vocation — bishop, priest, deacon, religious, lay — cooperates in building up the Mystical Body of Christ.

And so, amid all that troubles the human heart — violence, confusion, division, loneliness — Christ speaks again: *"Do not let your hearts be troubled."* He does not offer escape, but communion. Not an ideology, but a person. *"I am the Way, and the Truth, and the Life."*

He has gone ahead to prepare a place for us, and He sends His Spirit so that we may prepare the world for His return — not with fear, but with faith; not with resignation, but with joy.

Dear brothers and sisters, this Easter season proclaims that we are not orphans. Christ has not left us. He remains the Way we walk, the Truth we believe, and the Life that now lives in us.

Let us follow Him with courage, build upon Him with love, and serve through Him with peace — until the day we see the face of the Father in the light of glory.

"You now are the body of Christ, and individually members of it." (1 Cor 12:27)

Sixth Sunday of Easter

As the Easter season continues to unfold, the Church gently turns our gaze toward Pentecost. The Risen Christ, who once appeared in the garden and the upper room, now begins to prepare His disciples for His abiding presence through the Holy Spirit. The discourse of this Sunday's Gospel—spoken in the shadow of the Passion—is radiant with Trinitarian promise.

When Jesus says, *"If you love me, you will keep my commandments,"* He is not establishing a mere moral code but revealing the interior structure of divine communion. Love and obedience are not opposites; they are two expressions of the same reality. The one who truly loves desires to remain within the will of the Beloved. The Catechism teaches, *"To love is to will the good of another,"* and, *"All moral life is summed up in the command to love God and neighbor."* (CCC §1766, §1970).

In this sense, obedience is not the suppression of freedom but its perfection, for it orders the will toward God, who is the supreme Good. Saint Augustine, preaching on the First Letter of John, unfolds this mystery: *"Love, and do what you will. If you are silent, be silent for love; if you speak, speak for love; if you correct, correct for love; if you spare, spare for love. Let the root of love be within; from this root nothing can spring but what is good."* (*In Epistolam Ioannis ad Parthos*, Tract. 7, 8; PL 35:2033).

To love as Christ loves is to enter the kenotic rhythm of His own life: the self-emptying of the Son who receives all from the Father and returns all in love. The commandments of Christ are not external impositions but the inner grammar of this love made visible in human life.

Jesus then reveals the next stage of the mystery: *"I will ask the Father, and He will give you another Advocate to be with you always, the Spirit of truth."* (Jn 14:16–17). The Greek term *Paraklētos*—one who is called alongside—conveys both comforter and defender. The Spirit is not simply a messenger or energy, but the living Love of God Himself proceeding from the Father and the Son, entering history to dwell within the human heart.

Saint Basil the Great contemplates this divine intimacy: *"Through the Spirit we become partakers of God. The Spirit prepares us for divinization, not by nature but by grace. He brings us into communion with the divine life."* (De Spiritu Sancto, IX.23; PG 32:109). The Spirit is thus the bridge between the transcendent and the immanent—the one who makes God not merely an object of faith, but an indwelling presence.

Saint Thomas Aquinas gives the metaphysical depth of this truth: *"The Holy Spirit proceeds as love, by which God loves Himself and loves us."* (ST I, q.37, a.1). The Spirit's very name is Love (*amor subsistens*), the personal bond of charity within the Trinity, now poured into the hearts of the faithful. To receive the Spirit is not to receive "something" from God, but God Himself—the divine communion that unites the Father and the Son.

In the Acts of the Apostles, we see this same mystery enacted sacramentally as Peter and John lay hands upon the baptized, and they receive the Holy Spirit. This gesture is not merely symbolic; it manifests the structure of the Church as the temple of the Spirit. The

Spirit animates, sanctifies, and sends. Where the Spirit is, there is mission; and where there is mission, there is communion.

The words *"I will not leave you orphans"* pierce to the heart of human longing. Every culture knows the ache of spiritual abandonment. Christ's promise reveals the inner dynamic of the Trinity: the Son returns to the Father not to depart, but to send the Spirit, who makes the divine life itself the interior principle of the believer. Saint Paul's words express it perfectly: *"The love of God has been poured into our hearts through the Holy Spirit who has been given to us."* (Rom 5:5).

This means that Christian existence is not simply ethical imitation but ontological participation. We live in the Spirit; we are drawn into the very circulation of divine charity. The moral life is therefore Eucharistic—it flows from the indwelling Spirit toward the self-offering love of Christ.

Saint Peter's exhortation in the second reading gains its full weight in this light: *"Always be ready to give an explanation to anyone who asks you for a reason for your hope."* (1 Pt 3:15). Hope is not optimism, but the theological assurance that divine life has entered the frailty of our humanity. The early Church did not spread through force or argument, but through the witness of believers who lived as adopted children of the Father and bearers of the Spirit's joy.

Our age, too, suffers a spiritual orphanhood—rootless, restless, and afraid. But Christ's word remains: *"I will not leave you orphans."* The Spirit does not remove suffering; He transfigures it from within. He teaches the soul to see in the Cross not abandonment, but divine intimacy.

This promise is renewed at every Eucharist. For it is here, in the quiet of bread and wine, that the Risen Lord fulfills His word: *"I will come to you."* The Holy Spirit makes the sacrifice of Christ present anew, not as repetition, but as participation. As the Catechism teaches: *"The Holy Spirit prepares the Church to encounter her Lord. He recalls and makes Christ manifest to the faith of the assembly."* (CCC §1092).

The Eucharist is the living Pentecost of the Church. Here, the Spirit unites heaven and earth, makes the Word flesh among us again, and transforms the faithful into what they receive. The Spirit who overshadowed Mary at the Incarnation now overshadows the altar at every Mass, conceiving Christ anew in His Mystical Body.

Thus, we are not orphans but heirs—temples of the Spirit, sons and daughters of the Father, and members of the Body of Christ. The indwelling of the Spirit is not an appendix to the Paschal Mystery; it is its fulfillment. The Cross opens the way, the Resurrection reveals the glory, and the Spirit communicates the life.

As the Easter season draws toward Pentecost, let us ask anew for this indwelling. Let us allow the Advocate to turn fear into faith, anxiety into peace, and isolation into communion. Let the Spirit who proceeds as Love renew the Church in love.

We are not abandoned. We are not forgotten. We are not orphans. The Paraclete is within us.

And where the Spirit dwells, there is Christ; and where Christ is, there is the Father.

In that indwelling communion lies the whole mystery of Christian life — the beginning of eternal life already present in us.

"Come, Holy Spirit, fill the hearts of Your faithful, and enkindle in them the fire of Your love."

Seventh Sunday of Easter

We stand, liturgically and theologically, between Ascension and Pentecost—between the glory of Christ's return to the Father and the fire of the Spirit's descent upon the Church. It is a sacred pause, a time of luminous waiting. The Church rests in the silence between two great movements of the same Paschal Mystery. And today's Gospel, drawn from the seventeenth chapter of Saint John, draws us into the beating heart of that mystery: the prayer of the Son to the Father—the High Priestly Prayer.

Jesus lifts His eyes to heaven and begins, *"Father, the hour has come; glorify your Son, that the Son may glorify you."* (Jn 17:1). The "hour" has been approaching throughout the Gospel, and now it is upon Him. Yet it is not simply the hour of suffering—it is the hour of glorification. The Cross is not merely an instrument of execution; it is the throne of divine love.

Saint Augustine, in his *Tractates on the Gospel of John*, comments with precision: *"He said not, 'Save me from this hour,' but 'Father, glorify your Son.' For in that very hour when He was crucified, He was glorified."* (*Tract. in Ioannem*, 104, 4; PL 35:1910). What appears to human eyes as humiliation is, in divine light, the revelation of glory.

The "hour" encompasses all—the Passion, Death, Resurrection, and Ascension of Christ form one continuous act of glorification. It is the movement by which the Son, sent from the Father, returns to the Father, carrying with Him our humanity. The eternal Word descends to take flesh, and having redeemed that flesh, He raises it into the very communion of the Trinity.

Christ's glorification, then, is not His escape from the world but the transfiguration of it. He is not a passive victim but the eternal High Priest, both priest and victim, who offers Himself in love for the world's salvation. The Cross is the altar upon which divine and human love meet and are made one.

Jesus continues: *"Now this is eternal life: that they may know You, the only true God, and Jesus Christ whom You have sent."* (Jn 17:3). This "knowing" is not the knowledge of the philosopher—it is the communion of the lover. It is not cognition but participation, not speculation but union.

Saint Thomas Aquinas writes: *"To know God is to be united to Him in loving understanding. Eternal life is nothing other than the perfect vision of God joined with love."* (ST I, q.12, a.1). For Aquinas, knowledge without love is incomplete, and love without knowledge is blind; but in the beatific knowing of the saints, intellect and will are one flame—the intellect seeing, the will rejoicing, both caught up into the life of God Himself.

Thus, when Jesus defines eternal life as knowing the Father through the Son, He reveals salvation as communion, not escape. The Gospel is not about flight from the world, but about the indwelling of God within the world, reconciling all things to Himself.

"I glorified You on earth," Christ continues, *"by accomplishing the work You gave Me to do."* (Jn 17:4). That work—the *opus consummatum*—is obedience unto death, the surrender of love that undoes the rebellion of Adam. The glory of God is not measured in conquest but in charity. The Cross, therefore, is not the failure of

divine power but its revelation. As Augustine so often said, "The humility of God is the greatest expression of His majesty."

The Church, in these days between Ascension and Pentecost, reflects this same rhythm. The first reading from the Acts of the Apostles shows the disciples gathered in the upper room with Mary, the Mother of Jesus. They are silent, prayerful, and united. Saint John Chrysostom remarks beautifully: *"They persevered in prayer, because they expected a great promise; and their unanimity was itself a sign that the Spirit who was to come would bind them together in one body."* (*Hom. in Acta Apostolorum*, 3; PG 60:33). The Church already breathes with the Spirit she awaits.

This time of waiting is not empty; it is fecund. It is a Marian silence—like the stillness of Nazareth before the Incarnation, or Calvary before the dawn. The same Spirit who overshadowed Mary now prepares to overshadow the Church.

Saint Peter, in the second reading, reminds the early Christians that this path of glory inevitably passes through suffering: *"If you are insulted for the name of Christ, blessed are you... if you suffer as a Christian, do not be ashamed, but glorify God because you bear that name."* (1 Pt 4:14–16). To share in the glory of the Risen Lord is to share in the pattern of His Passion.

Aquinas comments on this Pauline mystery with clarity: *"Christ merited glory not only for Himself, but for all His members; and thus the faithful are made conformable to His suffering, that they may be partakers of His glory."* (*ST III, q.49, a.1*). The Cross is not an obstacle to glory but its necessary form; the Church is glorified not in worldly success, but in fidelity to crucified love.

The final words of Christ's prayer in this section open a window onto divine intimacy: *"They were yours, and you gave them to me, and they have kept your word."* (Jn 17:6). In that single verse is the whole theology of grace. Humanity belongs first to the Father, is given to the Son, and is sanctified by the Spirit. We are not self-created beings struggling toward meaning; we are gifts exchanged within the eternal dialogue of Trinitarian love.

This giving and receiving between Father and Son is not functional—it is nuptial. The Church herself is born from this exchange, the Bride drawn from the pierced side of the Bridegroom. To belong to Christ is to be caught up into that self-giving circulation of love that is the life of God Himself.

The days between Ascension and Pentecost are, therefore, an icon of the Church's life in history: we live in the tension between Christ's departure and His abiding presence, between fulfillment and promise, between already and not yet. Like the apostles, we wait with Mary; like them, we persevere in prayer; like them, we long for the fire of the Spirit.

Christ has ascended, but He has not left us. He intercedes even now, His priestly prayer continuing in the heart of the Trinity. And soon, as He promised, the Advocate will come—the Spirit of truth, the bond of love, the light of holiness.

Until that day, the Church waits—not in fear, but in faith; not in silence alone, but in song; not in absence, but in expectation. For the glorified Christ still prays: *"Father, glorify your Son, that the Son may glorify you."* And that prayer—spoken once in the upper room—resounds forever in the liturgy of heaven and in the heart of the Church.

So let us wait with Mary. Let us persevere in the upper room of prayer. Let us live between Ascension and Pentecost with hearts open to the fire of divine love.

For soon, the Spirit will come—not merely upon us, but within us—and the High Priestly prayer of Christ will be fulfilled in His Body, the Church.

"Glory be to Him whose power working in us can do infinitely more than we can ask or imagine."

— *Ephesians 3:20*

Solemnity of the Ascension of the Lord

Today, the Easter season reaches its radiant summit—the Solemnity of the Ascension of the Lord. After forty days of appearances, the Risen Christ now ascends bodily into heaven. Yet, paradoxically, He does not leave us behind. He takes our humanity with Him.

Saint Leo the Great proclaims with majestic simplicity: *"The visible ascension of Christ is the foundation of our hope; for where the Head has gone before in glory, the Body is called to follow in hope."* (*Sermo 73, De Ascensione Domini*; PL 54:396)

The Ascension, therefore, is not the Lord's farewell—it is His enthronement. It is the moment when the human nature of Christ, once crucified, is exalted above all the heavens, seated at the right hand of the Father. What seems to be a departure is, in truth, the completion of His mission and the beginning of ours.

In Saint Matthew's Gospel, the Risen Christ stands on the mountain and declares: *"All authority in heaven and on earth has been given to me."* (Mt 28:18) The words echo Daniel's vision: *"To Him was given dominion and glory and kingship, that all peoples, nations, and languages should serve Him."* (Dan 7:14) The Ascension is the fulfillment of that prophecy—the moment when the Son of Man, who was humiliated in the flesh, is now glorified as Lord of heaven and earth.

Saint Augustine marvels at this mystery, writing: *"He did not abandon heaven when He came down to us, nor did He lose the human nature He took from us when He ascended again into heaven."* (*Sermon 263*, 1; PL 38:1202)

In this single movement, Christ reveals both His divinity and His humanity. He ascends not as a spirit released from the body, but as the Word made flesh, carrying that flesh—our flesh—into the heart of the Trinity.

Saint Thomas Aquinas explains this with characteristic clarity: *"Christ ascended by His own power; and this was fitting, since He is both God and man. As man He ascends; as God, He draws all things to Himself."* (STh III, q.57, a.3)

The Ascension, then, is not a departure but a glorification. It is the exaltation of human nature itself—the restoration and elevation of creation through the humanity of Christ. Our destiny is no longer bound to the earth; it is seated, already, "in the heavenly places in Christ Jesus" (Eph 2:6).

Saint Luke tells us that *"a cloud took Him from their sight."* (Acts 1:9) This is not the cloud of disappearance, but of divine presence. Throughout Scripture, the cloud is the sign of God's glory—the cloud that led Israel through the desert (Ex 13:21), the cloud that covered Sinai (Ex 24:15–18), the cloud that filled Solomon's Temple (1 Kgs 8:10–11). The same cloud now envelops the Risen Christ. The one who once "pitched His tent among us" (Jn 1:14) now enters the heavenly sanctuary, not as shadow, but in reality.

The angels' question to the disciples—*"Why do you stand looking up at the sky?"*—is not a reproach but a summons. It means: Do not cling to what was. The same Lord who ascended will come again. Until then, His Body—the Church—must continue His work.

That is why, on the mountain, Jesus gives the Great Commission: *"Go, therefore, and make disciples of all nations... and behold, I am with you always, until the end of the age."* (Mt 28:19–20) The One who departs in glory remains in sacramental presence. The Lord's going is also His staying.

Saint Paul, in the Letter to the Ephesians, prays that the eyes of our hearts may be enlightened, so that we may know "the hope to which He has called us, the riches of His glorious inheritance, and the immeasurable greatness of His power for us who believe." (Eph 1:18–19) This is the spiritual vision opened by the Ascension.

Hope, as the Catechism teaches, *"is the theological virtue by which we desire the kingdom of heaven and eternal life as our happiness, placing our trust in Christ's promises and relying not on our own strength, but on the help of the grace of the Holy Spirit."* (CCC §1817)

In the Ascension, Christ Himself becomes the object of that hope. He is our path, our High Priest, and our destination. The humanity He assumed is now the bridge between heaven and earth, the pledge of our future glory.

Our Lady, too, stands quietly in this mystery. Saint Luke tells us that after the Ascension, the apostles returned to Jerusalem and *"with one accord devoted themselves to prayer, together with Mary the mother of Jesus."* (Acts 1:14) The Church's first novena begins there—in prayerful expectation, Marian and apostolic, awaiting the descent of the Spirit.

We are not meant to be immobilized between Ascension and Pentecost. Like Mary and the apostles, we are to watch and pray— but also to prepare for mission. The risen and ascended Christ does not command us to look to the sky; He commands us to go into the world. His departure is the beginning of our apostolic life.

Saint Leo, in another Ascension sermon, reminds us: *"Christ's Ascension is our elevation; and the hope of the body is where the glory of the Head has gone before."* (*Sermon 74*, 1; PL 54:398)

On this glorious feast, we do not proclaim absence but presence—presence in power. Christ has not gone far; He has gone deep: deep into the heart of the Father, deep into the mystery of the Eucharist, deep into the life of His Church.

The Ascended Lord intercedes for us as our High Priest. He reigns for us as our King. He prepares a place for us as our Brother and Bridegroom. And in every Mass, the veil between heaven and earth grows thin—for where the Head has gone, the Body follows.

Let us, then, fix our hearts on the things that are above—not to escape the world, but to transform it with the hope of heaven. For the same Lord who ascended in glory still speaks to His Church: *"And behold, I am with you always, even to the end of the age."*

Pentecost

Fifty days after Easter, the Church stands once more in the Upper Room — no longer in fear, but in fire. The Holy Spirit, the promised Paraclete, descends from the Father through the Son, filling the world with divine life. What began at the dawn of creation with the Spirit hovering over the waters (Gen 1:2) is now completed in the new creation — the Spirit hovering over the Church.

The mystery of Pentecost is not merely the conclusion of Easter; it is its fullness. The Cross, Resurrection, and Ascension reach their purpose in this outpouring of the Spirit, through whom Christ's redeeming work becomes interior, ecclesial, and enduring. What began in one body on Calvary now extends through the Body of Christ — the Church — animated by the Spirit who is Lord and Giver of Life.

Saint Irenaeus bears witness to this profound truth: "Where the Church is, there is the Spirit of God; and where the Spirit of God is, there is the Church and every grace." (*Adversus Haereses* III, 24, 1)

The Church is not first an institution, but a communion in the Holy Spirit. The same Spirit who formed Christ in the womb of Mary now forms Christ within us. The same Spirit who descended upon the Apostles now descends upon the baptized, renewing the face of the earth.

Saint Luke describes Pentecost with the language of theophany: *"And suddenly there came from heaven a sound like the rush of a mighty wind, and it filled all the house where they were sitting."* (Acts 2:2)

This is the breath (ruach) of new creation, recalling the wind that swept over the waters in Genesis and the thunder and flame of Sinai (Ex 19:16–19). The old covenant was written on stone amid fire and fear; the new covenant is written on hearts amid fire and love.

Saint Thomas Aquinas sees this deliberate parallel and writes: "As the Law was given to the Jews fifty days after the Passover, so the Holy Spirit was given to the disciples fifty days after the Resurrection. The Old Law was given in fear; the New Law in love." (*Commentary on the Gospel of John*, ch. 14, lect. 3)

The tongues of fire resting upon the disciples reveal that grace now burns where fear once dwelt. Babel's confusion is reversed; languages divide no longer but converge in praise. The Spirit does not abolish diversity — He transfigures it into harmony.

Saint John Chrysostom exclaims in wonder: "What is the meaning of the tongues of fire? That the Gospel is for the whole world. That the Spirit is a fire which inflames hearts and burns away sin." (*Homily on Acts 2*; PG 60:32)

The Church, born of fire, is catholic from her first breath. The Spirit of truth does not produce uniformity but communion — unity in difference, love amid multiplicity. The Spirit gathers, sanctifies, and sends.

John's Gospel offers a quieter Pentecost on Easter evening. Jesus enters the locked room and *"breathed on them and said, 'Receive the Holy Spirit.'"* (Jn 20:22).

The Greek verb ἐνεφύσησεν (*emphysēsen*) appears only once in the New Testament — the same word used in Genesis 2:7, when God breathed into Adam the breath of life. The Risen Lord breathes a new creation — the Spirit of divine life and forgiveness.

The Catechism of the Catholic Church reflects on this moment: "On the evening of Easter, Jesus breathes on them and says, 'Receive the Holy Spirit.' In this breath, the Spirit is communicated and sins are forgiven." (*CCC* §731)

Here begins the sacramental life of the Church. The Spirit who hovered over Mary and filled the Apostles now breathes divine life through Baptism, renews sinners in Reconciliation, strengthens in Confirmation, and unites all in the Eucharist. The Spirit is not an optional consolation; He is the very soul of the Church.

Saint Augustine describes this mystery with luminous precision: "The Church was born from the side of Christ as He slept on the Cross, and the Holy Spirit now gives her life, as the soul gives life to the body." (*Sermon* 267, 4; PL 38:1223)

The Spirit, therefore, is both interior and expansive — uniting the faithful in love while sending them forth in mission. The Apostle Paul reminds us that "to each is given the manifestation of the Spirit for the common good." (1 Cor 12:7) Diversity of gifts, unity of life. The same Spirit who sanctifies within also propels outward.

Saint Thomas Aquinas again clarifies this double grace: "Just as the soul gives life to each member according to its function, so the Holy Spirit distributes His gifts to each believer for the edification of the whole body." (*STh* I-II, q. 68, a. 1)

Thus, the Spirit builds the Church not through efficiency or power, but through holiness — through gifts ordered toward love. The Spirit's work is not only inspiration but transformation: He conforms the believer to Christ crucified and risen.

Saint Paul tells us in Romans: *"We do not know how to pray as we ought, but the Spirit Himself intercedes with inexpressible groanings."* (Rom 8:26) Even our weakness becomes prayer when the Spirit prays within us. This is divine intimacy — the breath of God praying through the human heart.

Pentecost, then, is not a single day remembered, but a life to be lived. The Spirit continues to descend — in every sacrament, in every mission, in every prayer whispered in faith. The same wind that rushed through the Upper Room still moves through the Church. The same fire that burned upon the Apostles still burns in every act of love. The same voice that spoke to their hearts still calls us: Go.

Saint Irenaeus once said that "the glory of God is the living man, and the life of man is the vision of God." (*Adversus Haereses* IV, 20, 7). Pentecost reveals both truths — for through the Spirit, humanity lives, and in that life, God is glorified.

Let us therefore pray with renewed longing:

Come, Holy Spirit, fill the hearts of your faithful, and kindle in them the fire of your love. Send forth your Spirit, and they shall be created, and you shall renew the face of the earth.

May this Pentecost not be merely a memory but a mission; not a story of the past, but a fire for the present. For Christ is risen, the Spirit has come, and the Church is alive. Alleluia.

Trinity Sunday

Today, the Easter season culminates in adoration and awe before the deepest mystery of our faith: the mystery not merely *about* God, but *of* God Himself — the Father, the Son, and the Holy Spirit. The doctrine of the Trinity is not an intellectual abstraction but the revelation of divine life as love.

Saint Augustine, the most luminous of the Western Trinitarians, begins his *De Trinitate* with both humility and hope: "In no other subject is error more dangerous, or inquiry more laborious, or the discovery of truth more profitable." (*De Trinitate* I, 3, 5)

The mystery of the Trinity, then, is not a problem to be solved but a communion to be entered. The more we contemplate it, the more we are drawn into the life it reveals — the life of God who is Love.

Today's Gospel gives us the verse that Saint John Chrysostom called *the summary of the Gospel itself*: "God so loved the world that He gave His only Son, that whoever believes in Him should not perish but have eternal life." (Jn 3:16)

This single sentence reveals the entire mystery of the Trinity. The Father gives; the Son is given; and the gift itself — love poured out — is the Holy Spirit. The Father's act of begetting the Son from all eternity and of sending Him into the world are one movement of self-giving love.

Saint Gregory Nazianzen articulates this with crystalline precision: "The Father is the begetter and the emitter; the Son is the begotten; the Holy Spirit is the emission. We recognize one God in these three: one substance, one glory, one action." (*Orationes Theologicae* 20.6; PG 35:1072)

Here is no division of labor or hierarchy of power, but eternal reciprocity — one act of divine love in three Persons. The Father is not Father without the Son; the Son is not Son without the Father; and their mutual love is not impersonal energy but the Spirit who unites.

Thus, when the Gospel declares that "God so loved," it means that the inner life of God — His Trinitarian love — has overflowed into history. What God is in Himself, He shares with us.

The first reading from Exodus reveals this mystery in figure and promise. God reveals Himself to Moses as "merciful and gracious, slow to anger and rich in kindness and fidelity." (Ex 34:6)

Here already we glimpse not isolated power but relational love — the divine self-diffusion that will be unveiled fully in Christ and the Spirit.

Saint Irenaeus saw the outlines of Trinitarian revelation even in the Old Covenant: "The Father is the invisible of the Son, the Son is the visible of the Father. The Spirit prepares humanity for the Son, and the Son leads us to the Father." (*Adversus Haereses* IV, 20, 6)

Already in creation and covenant, God is at work as Trinity: the Father creating, the Son revealing, the Spirit sanctifying. Salvation history is nothing other than the extension of the eternal processions of the divine life into time.

Saint Augustine, following this revelation, sought to discern within the human person — created *imago Dei* — the reflection of the Trinity. In the soul, he saw the triad of *memoria, intellectus,* and *voluntas* — memory, intellect, and will — three faculties, yet one life.

But Augustine's most profound insight goes beyond psychology to love itself: "You see the Trinity if you see love." (*De Trinitate* VIII, 10, 14)

In other words, wherever true love exists — giver, receiver, and the gift itself — there is an image, however faint, of the divine life. The Trinity is not the cold geometry of divinity, but the warmth of eternal charity.

Saint Thomas Aquinas, following Augustine yet refining the mystery with metaphysical precision, teaches that we know the Trinity only because God Himself has spoken.

"What we know of the Trinity is what God has revealed to us: that the Son proceeds by way of the intellect, as Word; and the Holy Spirit proceeds by way of the will, as Love." (*Summa Theologiae* I, q. 27–36, passim)

The divine Word is the perfect expression of the Father's mind; the Holy Spirit is the perfect act of the Father's and Son's love. Thus, all of God's outward works — creation, redemption, sanctification — are the joint work of the three divine Persons, who act inseparably.

And yet, Aquinas adds with luminous simplicity: "Charity is the Holy Spirit dwelling in us." (*ST II-II*, q. 23, a. 2)

The life of grace, therefore, is nothing less than participation in the inner life of the Trinity — the Father loving us through the Son in the Spirit.

Saint Paul's benediction captures this truth with sublime brevity: "The grace of the Lord Jesus Christ, the love of God, and the communion of the Holy Spirit be with all of you." (2 Cor 13:13)

This is not a formula for farewell but a summary of the entire economy of salvation: the Father's love as source, the Son's grace as mediation, and the Spirit's communion as indwelling life.

This same mystery structures the Church and the Christian vocation. The Church is not simply a human society that worships a Triune God — she is the visible sacrament of the Trinity's own life. Her unity and diversity, her mission and holiness, all mirror the divine communion from which she springs.

Every liturgical act reveals this. Every prayer begins "In the name of the Father, and of the Son, and of the Holy Spirit." Every Eucharist is addressed to the Father, made present through the Son, and consecrated in the Spirit. The entire Christian life is a participation in the Trinitarian rhythm of self-giving love.

In a world fractured by division and competition, the Trinity stands as both mystery and model: unity without absorption, distinction without separation. Love does not erase the other; it makes communion possible.

The Catechism of the Catholic Church expresses this with astonishing beauty: "God Himself is an eternal exchange of love: Father, Son, and Holy Spirit; and He has destined us to share in that exchange." (*CCC* §221)

To live the Christian life, then, is to live Trinitarianly — to receive love, to return love, and to become love. The Trinity is not only what we adore, but what we are called to become: a communion of persons united in truth and charity.

Let us, then, adore the Father who creates and sends, the Son who reveals and redeems, and the Holy Spirit who sanctifies and unites. Let our lives, our parishes, and our hearts become icons of this divine communion — radiant with love, steadfast in unity, and open to the life that flows from the Trinity's eternal exchange.

In every sign of the Cross, we proclaim the deepest truth of the universe:

God is not solitude, but *communio*; not domination, but gift; not power, but love.

Glory be to the Father, and to the Son, and to the Holy Spirit — as it was in the beginning, is now, and ever shall be, world without end. Amen.

Solemnity of the Most Holy Body and Blood of Christ (Corpus Christi)

Today, on the Solemnity of the Most Holy Body and Blood of Christ, the Church pauses in awe before the mystery at her heart—the Holy Eucharist, the *Sacramentum Caritatis*, the sacrament of Christ Himself. Here, under the humble signs of bread and wine, is contained the true Body, Blood, Soul, and Divinity of our Lord Jesus Christ. We do not merely recall Him. We receive Him. And in receiving Him, we become what we consume—the Body of Christ given for the life of the world.

In the Gospel of John, Christ reveals with startling clarity: "I am the living bread that came down from heaven; whoever eats this bread will live forever; and the bread that I will give is my flesh for the life of the world." (Jn 6:51)

The crowd is scandalized, and rightly so. Jesus does not correct their literal understanding. Instead, He intensifies it: "Amen, amen, I say to you, unless you eat the flesh of the Son of Man and drink His blood, you do not have life within you." (Jn 6:53)

This is not metaphor; it is mystery. Not symbol, but substance. The Word who became flesh now gives that same flesh as food.

The *Catechism of the Catholic Church* expresses this perennial faith: "In the most Blessed Sacrament of the Eucharist, the Body and Blood, together with the Soul and Divinity, of our Lord Jesus Christ and, therefore, the whole Christ is truly, really, and substantially contained." (*CCC* §1374)

Christ is not merely present in spirit or by faith, but truly and substantially, under the appearances of bread and wine. This change—while the accidents remain—is what the Church calls *transubstantiation.*

The Fourth Lateran Council (1215) declared: "His Body and Blood are truly contained in the sacrament of the altar under the forms of bread and wine; the bread being transubstantiated into the Body, and the wine into the Blood, by the divine power." (*Lateran IV*, c. 1)

And the Council of Trent reaffirmed this with luminous precision: "By the consecration of the bread and wine, there takes place a change of the whole substance of the bread into the substance of the Body of Christ our Lord, and of the whole substance of the wine into the substance of His Blood. This change the holy Catholic Church has fittingly and properly called transubstantiation." (*Council of Trent*, Session XIII, ch. 4)

Saint Thomas Aquinas, the Church's greatest theologian of the Eucharist, clarified this mystery using Aristotelian categories of *substance* and *accidents*: "The substance of the bread and wine is changed into the Body and Blood of Christ, while the species of bread and wine remain." (*Summa Theologiae* III, q. 75, a. 4)

It is not that Christ is *with* the bread, or *in* the bread, but that what was bread is now wholly the Body of Christ, and what was wine is wholly His Blood. The change is real, total, and unique to this sacrament.

In his great hymn, Aquinas bows before the mystery: *"Adoro te devote, latens Deitas, quae sub his figuris vere latitas"* — "I devoutly adore You, hidden Deity, who truly lie hidden beneath these appearances."

From the dawn of the Church, the Fathers spoke with one voice concerning this mystery.

Saint Ignatius of Antioch, writing at the dawn of the second century, warned against the heretics who denied the Eucharistic reality: "They abstain from the Eucharist and from prayer because they do not confess that the Eucharist is the flesh of our Savior Jesus Christ." (*Letter to the Smyrnaeans* 6)

Saint Justin Martyr wrote to the Roman Emperor around the year 155: "We do not receive these as common bread or common drink; but as Jesus Christ, our Savior, made flesh for our salvation." (*First Apology* 66)

And Saint Cyril of Jerusalem exhorted his catechumens: "Since He Himself has declared and said of the bread, 'This is My Body,' who shall dare to doubt it? And when He has affirmed and said, 'This is My Blood,' who shall ever hesitate, saying it is not His Blood?" (*Mystagogical Catecheses* 4, 1)

The early Church never spoke of mere symbolism. The Eucharist was adored, consumed, and proclaimed as the living Christ. What the Church teaches today is what she has believed from the beginning.

Saint Paul teaches in today's epistle: "The cup of blessing that we bless, is it not a participation in the Blood of Christ? The bread that we break, is it not a participation in the Body of Christ? Because there is one bread, we who are many are one body, for we all partake of the one bread." (1 Cor 10:16–17)

The Eucharist not only signifies unity—it *creates* it. The Church's communion is both expressed and brought about in the Eucharist. As the Fathers said, *the Eucharist makes the Church*. Full Eucharistic communion, therefore, presupposes full doctrinal unity: one faith, one sacramental priesthood, one apostolic succession.

Saint Augustine expresses this mutual belonging beautifully: "If you are the Body of Christ and His members, then what is placed on the Lord's table is your own mystery. Be what you see, and receive what you are." (*Sermon* 272)

The Eucharist does not merely gather individuals; it fashions a people. It forms us into the ecclesial Body of Christ, alive with divine charity.

The Solemnity of Corpus Christi draws us into three dimensions of this mystery: adoration, transformation, and mission.

First, adoration: because the Eucharist is Christ Himself, our silence before the tabernacle is filled with awe. As Pope Saint John Paul II urged, we must rediscover "Eucharistic amazement," for in this sacrament "Jesus hides Himself so that He may be adored."

Second, transformation: the Eucharist does not change Christ into us; it changes us into Christ. Aquinas teaches that "this sacrament works the unity of the mystical body" (*ST* III, q. 79, a. 1). The communicant is conformed to what he receives.

Third, mission: to receive the Eucharist is to be sent. The same Lord who says, "This is My Body," also says, "Go." The sacrament that gathers us also sends us into the world—to be broken, poured out, and offered for others.

The Eucharist is the mystery of divine self-emptying and divine fullness united. It is the Cross made present, the Resurrection made near, the Trinity made tangible. It is Christ Himself, offered and adored.

Let us renew our faith with the words of the Church's ancient antiphon, composed by Aquinas for this very feast: "O sacred banquet, in which Christ is received, the memory of His Passion is renewed, the soul is filled with grace, and a pledge of future glory is given to us."

May we approach the altar not as spectators, but as worshippers; not as consumers, but as disciples; not as individuals, but as members of His Body. For the Lord who feeds us is the Lord who transforms us—and in Him, the world is renewed.

Solemnity of the Sacred Heart

Today, we are invited to draw near to the very heart of God—not figuratively, but truly. The Solemnity of the Sacred Heart is not a mere sentiment, nor a devotional ornament, but a revelation of the deepest mystery of divine love: God made flesh, whose Heart beats, bleeds, and burns eternally for us.

Saint John tells us: "Having loved His own who were in the world, He loved them to the end" (Jn 13:1). The Sacred Heart is this love "to the end"—a love that withholds nothing, that pours itself out even unto death, that continues to burn in glory.

In the first reading, Moses reminds Israel of God's electing love: "It was not because you are greater than all other nations that the Lord set His heart on you and chose you, but because the Lord loved you." (Deut 7:7–8)

God's love is not a response to worthiness. It is uncaused, faithful, and free. He loves because He is love. In Christ, that divine love takes on a human heart—the Heart of the Incarnate Word, in whom divine charity assumes human tenderness, emotion, and suffering.

Saint Augustine, meditating on this mystery, writes: "He loved us even when we did not exist; He made us that we might be, and He loved us so that we might not perish." (*In Epistolam Ioannis ad Parthos* Tractate 9.9)

This is what we contemplate today: not an abstraction, but a Heart that reveals the invisible God through visible, crucified love.

In today's Gospel, Jesus invites the weary: "Come to me, all you who labor and are burdened, and I will give you rest. Take my yoke

upon you, and learn from me, for I am meek and humble of heart."
(Mt 11:28–29)

This is the only place in Scripture where Jesus explicitly describes His own Heart. And what does He reveal? Not grandeur or power, but humility and gentleness. His meekness is not weakness—it is divine strength expressed through surrender.

On the Cross, this Heart is pierced by the soldier's lance. Saint John testifies: "One of the soldiers pierced His side with a spear, and immediately blood and water flowed out." (Jn 19:34)

The Fathers saw in this the birth of the Church. Saint Augustine teaches: "The Evangelist used a well-chosen word. He did not say that the soldier struck His side or wounded it or anything else, but that he *opened* it, so that thereby the door of life might be opened—whence flowed the sacraments of the Church." (*Tractate on John* 120.2)

The blood and water signify Baptism and the Eucharist—new birth and nourishment. From the open side of Christ flows the life of grace that transforms humanity.

Saint Thomas Aquinas explains that "the water denotes justification through baptism, and the blood denotes spiritual refreshment through the Eucharist." (*ST* III, q. 66, a. 3, ad 3). The Heart of Christ, then, is the fountainhead of all sacramental life. From it, the Church is born; in it, she abides.

The second reading reminds us: "God is love, and whoever remains in love remains in God and God in him." (1 Jn 4:16)

The Sacred Heart is not simply an image of affection—it is the visible sign of the invisible Trinity. Pope Pius XII wrote in *Haurietis Aquas*: "The Heart of Jesus is the principal sign and symbol of that love with which the divine Redeemer loves the eternal Father and all human beings." (*Haurietis Aquas*, §54)

In this Heart, we glimpse the eternal circulation of love between Father, Son, and Holy Spirit, poured out into time for our redemption. The devotion to the Sacred Heart, then, is not peripheral—it is Trinitarian, Christological, and ecclesial.

Saint Margaret Mary Alacoque, to whom Christ revealed the depths of this mystery, heard these words from the Lord: "Behold this Heart which has so loved men that it has spared nothing, even to exhausting and consuming itself, in order to testify its love; and in return, I receive from the greater part only ingratitude." (*Autobiography*, Part I, §86)

The devotion that began in her monastery at Paray-le-Monial is not a private spirituality; it is the Church's call to reparation—to console the Heart that still suffers from indifference and sin.

To live from the Sacred Heart is to allow our own hearts to be reshaped—meek instead of proud, merciful instead of vengeful, constant instead of capricious. Saint Catherine of Siena once prayed: "Sweet Jesus, my Love, I see no way but through Your opened Heart." (*Letter 26*)

That is the way of holiness: to enter through the wound of love and dwell within divine mercy.

In the Eucharist, the Heart of Christ beats still. The same love that bled on Calvary is present under sacramental signs. Saint Thomas Aquinas reminds us: "This sacrament is the memorial of Our Lord's Passion, containing Christ Himself who suffered for us." (*ST* III, q. 73, a. 4)

The Sacred Heart is thus Eucharistic: it is both the reality we adore and the love that transforms us. The Eucharist draws us into that same act of self-giving, until our own hearts are configured to His.

Pope Benedict XVI beautifully expressed this link in *Deus Caritas Est*: "The pierced Heart of Jesus is the source from which flows the true spirit of service and self-giving. In the Eucharist, adoration becomes union." (*DCE*, §14)

To approach this Heart is to approach the Eucharistic mystery— to adore, to receive, to be changed.

The Heart of Christ is the revelation of the Father's love, the dwelling of the Spirit, the source of the Church's life. To venerate it is to enter into that living exchange of love that defines the Trinity itself.

Saint Paul gives voice to this transformation: "I live, now not I, but Christ lives in me." (Gal 2:20)

This is the goal of devotion to the Sacred Heart: not mere emotion, but participation—Christ's love lived within us.

Let us therefore draw near with trust. Let us adore in silence before the pierced Heart that continues to pour out mercy. Let our own hearts be reshaped into His likeness—gentle, humble, burning with divine charity. And as we receive the Eucharist, the living Heart of Christ given for the life of the world, may our final prayer be the Church's ancient invocation:

Sacred Heart of Jesus, have mercy on us.

Feast of the Immaculate Heart of Mary

Today the Church, having just adored the Sacred Heart of Jesus, turns with love and reverence to the Immaculate Heart of His Mother. The two feasts are inseparable: the Son's Heart, pierced for love of the world, and the Mother's Heart, pierced in union with His. Both reveal not sentimentality, but theology—love made flesh, suffering transfigured into redemption.

This feast does not celebrate a mere symbol of tenderness; it reveals the mystery of a human heart perfectly attuned to the will of God. As Pope St. John Paul II once said, *"In Mary's Heart, the entire history of salvation is inscribed, and the covenant of God with humanity reaches its perfection."* (Homily, Fatima, May 13, 1982)

Saint Luke tells us twice in his Gospel: "Mary kept all these things, pondering them in her heart." (Lk 2:19; cf. 2:51)

The Greek verb *diētereō*—"to keep"—means more than simple remembrance. It signifies guarding, cherishing, meditating. Mary's heart is not passive memory but active contemplation. She holds together the mysteries of her Son—His birth, His words, His wounds—and interprets them in the silence of faith.

Saint Augustine gives us the key to this mystery: "She conceived Him in her heart before she conceived Him in her womb." (*De sancta virginitate*, 3; PL 40:398)

Before the Incarnation took place in her body, it was already accepted in her heart. The Annunciation is the moment when divine grace meets perfect human freedom, and Mary's "Fiat"—her yes—is the fullest act of faith ever uttered by a creature. Her Immaculate

Heart is the dwelling where the Word was first believed before He was seen.

Saint Thomas Aquinas teaches that faith perfects the intellect by ordering it to the truth of God (ST II-II, q. 4, a. 1). In Mary, that perfection reaches its summit: she is the one in whom faith and charity coincide without division, whose intellect is illumined by grace and whose will rests entirely in love.

Simeon's prophecy pierces the Gospel narrative like a blade: "And a sword will pierce through your own soul also." (Lk 2:35)

This is not only a prediction of sorrow—it is a revelation of participation. The sword that pierces Mary's soul is the same that opens her Son's side. She suffers not beside Him but with Him; she enters into the mystery of co-suffering love.

Saint Bernard of Clairvaux contemplates this moment with profound realism: "Truly, O Blessed Mother, a sword has pierced your soul. For only by passing through your soul could it pierce the flesh of your Son." (*Sermon on the Twelve Stars*, 14; PL 183:437)

Mary's compassion—literally, her "suffering-with"—reveals the depth of her union with Christ's redemptive love. She is not a passive observer of Calvary but the New Eve standing beside the New Adam, offering her maternal consent even in agony.

The Church calls her Heart *immaculate* because it is entirely transparent to God. From the first moment of her conception, she was preserved free from original sin by the merits of her Son. The Catechism teaches clearly: "By the grace of God, Mary remained free of every personal sin her whole life long." (CCC §493)

Purity here means not mere moral innocence but total integrity of love. Her heart is whole, undivided, and fully ordered toward God—the living image of the soul restored by grace.

Saint John Henry Newman once reflected that "Mary's sinlessness is not mere freedom from evil, but the fullness of grace." (*Discourses to Mixed Congregations*, 1849) Her Immaculate Heart, therefore, is the human echo of the divine Heart of Christ—a created participation in that uncreated charity which is the Holy Spirit Himself.

Saint Irenaeus had already glimpsed this mystery in the second century: "The knot of Eve's disobedience was loosed by the obedience of Mary; for what the virgin Eve had bound by unbelief, the Virgin Mary loosed by faith." (*Adversus Haereses*, III.22.4; PG 7:959)

The Immaculate Heart is not an isolated devotion; it is a theological sign of the Church herself—the Bride of Christ made immaculate by His grace.

To venerate the Immaculate Heart of Mary is to contemplate what the Church is called to become. She is the first disciple, the first contemplative, the first to believe, and the first to share in her Son's redemptive suffering. In her we see the form of ecclesial holiness: receptive, obedient, fruitful, and faithful.

As Pope Benedict XVI explained: "Mary's Heart, fully open to the will of God, is the image of the Church who listens, guards, and brings forth the Word." (*Homily at Fatima*, May 13, 2010)

The Church, like Mary, must keep and ponder, must speak her fiat amid the Cross, must treasure divine mysteries in silence and hope.

Consecration to the Immaculate Heart, then, is not an escape from the world but a deeper immersion into the mystery of divine love—a participation in the interior life of Mary, who in turn draws us always to Jesus.

Saint John Eudes, who first promoted this feast in the seventeenth century, wrote: "The Heart of Mary and the Heart of Jesus are but one Heart—the same love, the same compassion, the same will." (*Le Cœur Admirable de la Très Sainte Mère de Dieu*, Book I, ch. 5)

In contemplating her Heart, we are drawn into His.

The Immaculate Heart of Mary is the silence that listens, the faith that endures, the love that does not fail. It is the maternal heart of the Church, in which the mysteries of Christ are continually treasured, shared, and borne into the world.

To live this mystery is to allow our hearts to be purified and enlarged—to love as she loved, to believe as she believed, to suffer as she suffered.

Let us, then, draw near to her today. Let us entrust to her all that is wounded, fearful, and divided within us. Let her Heart teach us how to love without reserve, how to ponder without despair, how to stand at the Cross without losing hope.

For the Heart of Mary beats forever in perfect harmony with the Heart of her Son—pierced yet radiant, immaculate yet maternal, silent yet speaking the eternal word of love.

Immaculate Heart of Mary, pray for us. Lead us always to the Heart of your Son.

Solemnity of the Nativity of Saint John the Baptist

Today the Church celebrates one of her most luminous solemnities—the birth of Saint John the Baptist. Alongside the Blessed Virgin Mary, he is the only saint whose nativity is commemorated liturgically. The date itself is symbolic: six months before Christmas, when the sun begins to wane, because John was sent to herald the Light that would never set. His very birth is prophecy; his life, a sermon; his death, a seal upon truth.

The people of Zechariah and Elizabeth's village asked in wonder, "What, then, will this child be?" (Lk 1:66)

That question is not curiosity—it is revelation. For in the mystery of this birth, the entire story of salvation advances. A barren woman conceives; a mute father speaks; and the child who will prepare the way for the Lord enters the world. From his conception, John's life bears the imprint of divine election. The prophet Isaiah's words, proclaimed in the first reading, could be spoken by John himself: "The Lord called me from the womb, from my mother's womb he gave me my name." (Is 49:1)

John stands at the hinge of the covenants. He is, as Jesus Himself says, "more than a prophet" (Mt 11:9)—the bridge between the long night of expectation and the dawn of redemption. His task is not to announce an idea, but a person: "Behold, the Lamb of God, who takes away the sin of the world!" (Jn 1:29)

Saint Augustine, preaching on this mystery, captured John's unique vocation: "John was the voice, but the Lord was the Word.

The voice passes away, but the Word remains. Take away the word, and what is the voice? When it conveys the word, it is heard and ceases." (*In Iohannis Evangelium Tractatus*, 293.3; PL 38:1328)

John's greatness lies in his very disappearance. His voice fades as the Word speaks. His mission ends when the Light appears. The rhythm of their feasts reflects this: John is born when the days begin to grow shorter, Christ when they begin to lengthen. As John himself says, with beautiful humility: "He must increase; I must decrease." (Jn 3:30)

This is not only the pattern of his life—it is the pattern of discipleship. Every Christian is called to live this rhythm of diminishing self and increasing Christ. John's greatness, therefore, is the greatness of self-forgetful fidelity.

Saint Bede the Venerable wrote of him: "John showed in his conduct what he preached by word. He called others to repentance, and by his example, he strengthened them for it." (*Homilies on the Gospels*, 2.17; PL 94:56)

The austerity of his life—his desert solitude, rough garment, and simple food—was not mere asceticism, but prophecy. His entire being was ordered toward his mission: to prepare a people for the Lord.

Saint Thomas Aquinas reflects on this sanctity in his Commentary on Matthew, noting that John was holy even before birth: "He was sanctified in the womb, illumined by divine grace before he saw the light, and he died not for denying Christ, but for defending the law of God." (*Commentary on Matthew*, ch. 14, lect. 1)

John's martyrdom is therefore the perfection of his mission. The one who proclaimed the truth in the wilderness continued to proclaim it in Herod's court and paid with his life. He was the final prophet of the Old Covenant and the first martyr of the New. In him, the prophetic voice finds its ultimate expression: a word that bears witness to the Truth even unto death.

His courage, however, was inseparable from humility. When the people began to suspect that he might be the Messiah, John refused the title: "I am not the Christ... I am the voice of one crying out in the wilderness." (Jn 1:20, 23)

In that humility lies his sanctity. As Augustine says elsewhere, "He understood that he was the lamp, but not the light." (*Sermon* 293.4) The lamp burns to its end so that the true Light may shine.

The Church venerates John not only as prophet and martyr but as model. His vocation continues in us. The question once asked at his birth—"What, then, will this child be?"—is asked anew at every baptismal font, every ordination, every act of vocation discernment. What will this child of God become? A voice or an echo? A witness or a bystander?

John's life offers the pattern: clarity of truth, humility of spirit, and courage of witness. He did not flatter power or compromise morality. He called sin by its name, yet pointed always to mercy—to "the Lamb of God who takes away the sin of the world."

Our age, like Herod's, is fascinated and repelled by such voices. The Church's mission, however, remains unchanged: to prepare the way for the Lord in hearts grown indifferent, to make straight His paths in a wilderness of confusion. The more Christ increases, the more humanity is restored. The more the Church humbles herself before the truth, the brighter her witness becomes.

Today's feast, therefore, is not nostalgia—it is vocation. We celebrate the birth of a prophet whose very life explains the Gospel he preached. He is the friend of the Bridegroom who rejoices to hear the Bridegroom's voice. He is the herald who becomes the silence before the Word. He is the burning lamp, consumed in order to illuminate others.

Let us ask, through the intercession of Saint John the Baptist, for the grace to bear his likeness—to be courageous in truth, humble in service, and steadfast in witness. May our lives, too, become a voice crying in the wilderness of this world:

"Prepare the way of the Lord, make straight His paths." (Lk 3:4)

Solemnity of Saints Peter and Paul

Today the Church lifts up two great pillars of her life and mission: Saint Peter and Saint Paul — the fisherman and the scholar, the shepherd and the herald, the rock and the trumpet of God. Their personalities could not have been more different, yet the Church celebrates them together because in their union we perceive the fullness of her mystery — both stable and dynamic, both contemplative and missionary, both hierarchical and charismatic.

These two apostles embody what Saint Augustine called *duae lampades ardentes in uno lumine*, "two blazing lamps united in one light" (*Sermon 295*). Each burns with the same fire of Christ, yet with distinct brilliance. Peter signifies the enduring foundation of the Church; Paul signifies her ever-expanding mission. Both died in Rome, sanctifying the heart of the Empire and sealing their witness with blood.

Christ's words to Peter resound with singular solemnity: "You are Peter, and upon this rock I will build my Church, and the gates of hell shall not prevail against it." (Mt 16:18)

In these words, the Lord institutes not a personal privilege but a permanent office — the Petrine ministry, which guarantees the visible unity and doctrinal fidelity of the Church. Saint Leo the Great teaches that this office endures through the successors of Peter: "The care of the universal Church rests upon Peter's see, for the primacy remains; the form of Peter's service passes into his successors." (*Sermon 3 on the Anniversary of His Ordination*, 2)

Peter's humanity — his impulsiveness, his fear, his denial — becomes the very instrument of grace. The rock is not Peter's strength but Christ's mercy working in Peter's weakness. The Church's unity, therefore, is not built upon perfection but upon faith, the confession Peter made when he declared, "You are the Christ, the Son of the living God." (Mt 16:16) In that confession, the Church finds her foundation; in that faith, she stands firm amid the storms of history.

Yet where Peter gathers and guards, Paul goes forth and proclaims. If Peter's vocation is stability, Paul's is motion. The Gospel, Paul insists, cannot remain confined: "Woe to me if I do not preach the Gospel!" (1 Cor 9:16)

Saint John Chrysostom calls him *the trumpet of heaven*: "The voice of Paul rang out louder than thunder; it went out to the ends of the earth, shaking the foundations of idolatry." (*Homily 32 on Acts*)

Paul's mission was to open the covenant to the nations, to translate the mystery of Israel's Messiah into the language of the Gentiles. He is the Church's first theologian — not because he speculated abstractly, but because he lived from revelation, writing under the fire of the Spirit. In his letters, theology becomes proclamation, and proclamation becomes doxology.

In the second reading today, Paul's words anticipate his martyrdom: "I have fought the good fight, I have finished the race, I have kept the faith." (2 Tim 4:7)

"The Lord stood by me and gave me strength, so that through me the message might be fully proclaimed." (2 Tim 4:17) Here, at the end of his life, Paul recognizes what Peter would also learn — that all apostolic fruitfulness flows from participation in the Cross. The apostle's glory is not in success but in fidelity.

Saint Thomas Aquinas reflects on this paradox: "The Church is founded on faith and confession — faith in the divinity of Christ, and confession unto martyrdom. This is the meaning of Peter's and Paul's witness." (*Catena Aurea on Matthew 16:18*)

Without Peter, the Church would dissolve into fragmentation. Without Paul, she would wither into self-enclosure. The Lord, in His providence, joined these two lives so that the Church might be both grounded and going forth, both rooted in unity and radiant in mission.

Their relationship was not without tension. Paul recounts that he "opposed Peter to his face" at Antioch (Gal 2:11), reminding us that ecclesial communion is not uniformity but a communion purified through truth and charity. In the end, both apostles were reconciled in the same confession of Christ and united in the same death — Peter crucified upside down, Paul beheaded by the sword. Rome became not the grave of their rivalry but the cradle of their unity.

Their martyrdom reveals two facets of the one mystery of the Church. Peter's death signifies pastoral fidelity, the laying down of one's life for the flock. Paul's death signifies apostolic zeal, the offering of one's life for the Gospel. Together, they embody what the Church must always be: *ecclesia una, sancta, catholica et apostolica* — one, holy, catholic, and apostolic.

In every age, the Church is tempted to separate what God has joined: to prize structure over Spirit, or to exalt freedom over fidelity. Yet the Spirit unites these dimensions in harmony, not opposition. Saint John Paul II expressed this beautifully: "The Church is both Petrine and Marian, both hierarchical and charismatic, because she is modeled on the mystery of the Incarnation." (*Redemptoris Mater*, §27) The same is true of her apostolic life: she is both Petrine and Pauline — united, yet diverse in charism and mission.

On this solemnity, therefore, we pray for both graces: For Petrine fidelity — steadfast communion with the successor of Peter, our Holy Father Pope Leo XIV, who, like his predecessors, bears the weight of unity on his shoulders. And for Pauline fervor — missionary courage, theological depth, and evangelizing zeal that dares to speak Christ into the heart of every culture.

The Church must be both firm and free, faithful and fruitful, guarding the deposit of faith while proclaiming it anew in every generation. The Spirit who filled Peter and Paul continues to animate the Body of Christ, shaping pastors who shepherd and apostles who go forth, theologians who preach and martyrs who witness.

Their feast is not simply a remembrance of past heroes but a call to renewed discipleship. To stand with Peter is to confess Christ with the Church. To walk with Paul is to bear that confession into the world. To live their unity is to live the mystery of the Church herself — one faith, one Lord, one baptism, one Spirit, one mission.

Let us then ask their intercession: that Peter's steadfast faith may strengthen our communion, that Paul's apostolic zeal may inflame our hearts, and that together, we may glorify the one Lord whom they both served unto death — Jesus Christ, the Son of the living God.

Assumption of the Blessed Virgin Mary

Today, the Church throughout the world lifts her eyes and heart toward heaven in wonder and joy. We celebrate the Assumption of the Blessed Virgin Mary — a dogma solemnly defined by Pope Pius XII in *Munificentissimus Deus* (1950), yet believed and celebrated from the earliest centuries: that Mary, at the end of her earthly life, was taken up body and soul into heavenly glory.

This is not a feast only about Mary; it is a feast about us. In her, we behold the perfection of what the Church is called to be. As the Second Vatican Council teaches in *Lumen Gentium*: "The Mother of Jesus, in the glory which she possesses in body and soul in heaven, is the image and beginning of the Church as it is to be perfected in the world to come. Likewise, she shines forth on earth until the day of the Lord shall come, a sign of sure hope and solace to the pilgrim People of God." (*Lumen Gentium*, §68)

Saint Paul proclaims: "Christ has been raised from the dead, the firstfruits of those who have fallen asleep." (1 Corinthians 15:20). But after the firstfruits, there must follow the harvest. In Mary, the Church sees the first of those redeemed who already share fully in the Resurrection of her Son. She who bore Life Himself could not be held by the corruption of death.

Saint John Damascene, preaching in the eighth century, proclaimed: "It was fitting that she, who had kept her virginity intact in childbirth, should keep her own body free from all corruption even after death. It was fitting that she, who had carried the Creator as a child at her breast, should dwell in the divine tabernacles. It was fitting that she, who was espoused by the Father, should live in the heavenly chambers." (*Homily on the Dormition of Mary*, II.14; PG 96, 741)

Mary's Assumption is not an arbitrary privilege, nor merely a reward. It is the natural flowering of her Immaculate Conception, her perfect union with Christ's redemptive work, and her fidelity at the Cross. In her glorification, the victory of Christ reaches its most perfect expression in a human creature.

The first reading from Revelation offers a cosmic vision: "A woman clothed with the sun, with the moon under her feet, and on her head a crown of twelve stars." (Revelation 12:1)

The Fathers saw in this woman both Mary and the Church — inseparably united. She is the New Eve, the Mother of the living, the figure of the Church who receives, conceives, and bears Christ into the world.

Saint Irenaeus wrote: "As Eve, having disobeyed, became the cause of death both to herself and to all the human race, so Mary, being obedient, became the cause of salvation both to herself and the whole human race." (*Adversus Haereses*, III.22.4)

Saint Bernard of Clairvaux expressed this mystery with sublime clarity: "Through Mary, the neck of the Body, the gifts of the Head are communicated to His members." (*Sermo de Aquaeductu*, §4; PL 183:441B)

In the Assumption, we behold what grace accomplishes. The "lowly handmaid of the Lord" (Luke 1:38), who said her fiat in Nazareth, is now exalted in glory. Her *Magnificat* is fulfilled: "He has looked upon the lowliness of His handmaid... He has cast down the mighty from their thrones and has lifted up the lowly." (Luke 1:48, 52)

The mystery of the Assumption speaks profoundly to our age —
an age that forgets the sacredness of the body and the reality of
heaven. Mary's glorification proclaims that salvation is not merely
spiritual. The body is not a prison to be escaped, but a temple destined for resurrection. In her, humanity's full dignity is revealed: redeemed, transfigured, and glorified.

The *Catechism of the Catholic Church* affirms: "The Assumption
of the Blessed Virgin is a singular participation in her Son's Resurrection and an anticipation of the resurrection of other Christians."
(*CCC*, §966)

Saint Thomas Aquinas, reflecting on this fittingness, wrote: "As
death entered into the world through Eve, so through Mary life has
returned." (*Expositio super Ave Maria*, §5)

Mary's body, which bore the Incarnate Word, was not to see corruption. The same divine power that raised Christ from the dead
raised her, uniting her wholly to her Son in glory.

Saint Germanus of Constantinople, in his homily on the Dormition, prayed: "You have been exalted above the choirs of angels, yet
you have not departed from those who live on earth; rather, you remain close to all who call upon you." (*Homily I on the Dormition*, PG
98:352)

Thus, Mary's exaltation does not distance her from us — it draws
her nearer. She who is assumed into heaven continues to intercede
for her children, guiding the Church on her pilgrim journey.

The Solemnity of the Assumption is not a day of abstraction but
of promise fulfilled. The earth has yielded its most precious fruit;
heaven has received its Queen. The Church looks upward not in

nostalgia, but in hope. For in her, the final destiny of redeemed humanity is already realized.

Saint Augustine wrote of Christ: "The resurrection of our Head is the hope of our own resurrection." (*Enarrationes in Psalmos*, 88.5)

Therefore, Mary's Assumption is our hope — the assurance that what God has accomplished in her, He desires to accomplish in us. Her glory is not distant; it is our vocation. Her *Magnificat* is our song.

Let us lift our eyes to where she has gone before us, and follow her path of faith, humility, and love.

Mary, assumed into heaven, pray for us — that we may one day share the glory of your Son.

Solemnity of All Saints

Today the Church lifts her eyes to the heavenly Jerusalem, to that "great multitude which no one could count," clothed in white robes, standing before the Lamb. The Solemnity of All Saints is not a celebration of the past—it is a glimpse into our future, a joyful vision of the final goal of every human life. It is a feast of divine hope and human fulfillment.

The saints are not superhuman. They are the men and women who allowed the grace of God to shape them into something beautiful, something eternal.

Saint John tells us in the second reading: *"We shall be like him, for we shall see him as he is."* (1 John 3:2)

This is the deepest truth of the saints: they are those who have been transformed by the vision of God, those who have allowed His light to penetrate their entire being.

To be a saint, then, is not primarily to perform great deeds, but to allow the Beatitudes to be lived in one's body—*to be poor in spirit, to mourn, to hunger and thirst for righteousness, to be pure of heart*—and to trust that God's glory is made perfect in our weakness.

This means that sanctity is not optional; it is the Church's very vocation. Today's feast is not merely about canonized saints, but also the hidden saints, the ones unknown to the world but radiant in the eyes of God—"those who have washed their robes in the blood of the Lamb."

The Beatitudes, proclaimed in today's Gospel, are the blueprint of this holiness. They turn the world upside down—but they describe the shape of Christ's life and the life of all the saints.

Today's feast teaches us to view life not through the narrow lens of comfort, success, or visibility—but through the lens of eternity. When Jesus says, *"Blessed are you when they persecute you... Rejoice and be glad"*, He is not offering sentimental piety. He is revealing the logic of heaven.

The Book of Revelation gives us a heavenly vision—but not of the elite. It is a vision of an uncountable multitude. This should give us courage. The path to sanctity is open to all, even if narrow. It is a way of suffering love, of hidden fidelity, of clinging to Christ in the dark.

The saints are not simply intercessors—they are our future selves. That is why we venerate them and why we are inspired by them. The Catechism teaches: *"The Church on earth is endowed already with a sanctity that is real though imperfect."* (CCC §825)

In other words, the saints remind us of what is possible. They remind us that God is faithful, that grace is powerful, and that the Church, despite her wounds, still gives birth to holiness in every age. The drama of salvation is ongoing—that every life has a role in the divine play.

On this Solemnity of All Saints, let us renew our vocation to holiness. Let us draw near to the saints—known and unknown—so that we may learn how to follow Christ more closely. Let us take up the Beatitudes again, not as poetic ideals, but as the portrait of Christ, and the pattern of our own future in Him. Let us, in the words of today's psalm, "seek the face of the Lord," for that face is radiant in the faces of the saints. And let us never forget that our names, too, are written in heaven—if only we allow God to write our story with His grace.

Commemoration of All the Faithful Departed (All Souls' Day)

Today, the Church turns her heart and intercession toward those who have died in Christ and yet await the fullness of their redemption. If All Saints' Day proclaims the glory of heaven, then All Souls' Day draws us into the mystery of mercy, purification, and hope that does not disappoint.

This is a day filled with a tender seriousness. We come not merely to remember the dead but to pray for them—because in the communion of the Church, our prayers matter. They are acts of love that reach beyond death, for love in Christ never dies.

The Church teaches that every human life will reach its consummation in what tradition calls *the Four Last Things*: death, judgment, heaven, and hell. Death is not annihilation but transition—the doorway through which every soul must pass. The *Catechism of the Catholic Church* teaches:

"Death is the end of man's earthly pilgrimage, of the time of grace and mercy which God offers him so as to work out his earthly life in keeping with the divine plan and to decide his ultimate destiny." (*CCC* §1013)

At the moment of death, the soul is separated from the body and faces the particular judgment of God. "It is appointed for men to die once, and after that comes judgment" (Hebrews 9:27). For some, that judgment reveals a soul perfected in charity—ready to behold the face of God. For others, it discloses a will turned away from divine love, a tragic rejection of mercy. But for many souls, the judgment reveals a heart in friendship with God, yet still imperfectly purified. These enter what the Church calls *Purgatory*—a mystery not of despair, but of burning love.

The *Catechism* explains: "The Church gives the name Purgatory to this final purification of the elect, which is entirely different from the punishment of the damned. The faithful who have died in God's grace and friendship, but still imperfectly purified, are indeed assured of their eternal salvation; but after death they undergo purification, so as to achieve the holiness necessary to enter the joy of heaven." (*CCC* §1030–1031)

Saint Catherine of Genoa, who experienced profound insight into this mystery, wrote: "The greatest suffering of souls in Purgatory is the delay in seeing God; the greatest joy is the certainty that they will see Him, and that His pure love is working to make them worthy of it." (*Treatise on Purgatory*, ch. 1)

Thus, the fire of Purgatory is not the fire of vengeance, but the fire of divine love—the flame of Christ's gaze that purifies the soul until it is fully itself, fully capable of joy.

Why, then, do we pray for the dead? Because love unites what death divides. We believe, as Scripture teaches, that "it is a holy and wholesome thought to pray for the dead, that they may be loosed from their sins" (2 Maccabees 12:46). The communion of saints does not end with the grave. Those on earth, those being purified, and those in heaven form one living body in Christ.

Saint John Chrysostom urged the faithful: "Let us help and commemorate them. If Job's sons were purified by their father's sacrifice, why would we doubt that our offerings for the dead bring them some consolation? Let us not hesitate to help those who have died and to offer our prayers for them." (*Homily on 1 Corinthians 41.5; PG 61, 361*)

Our prayers, then, are not symbolic gestures but real acts of mercy. When we offer the Holy Mass for the departed, when we recite the Rosary, light a candle, or visit the cemetery, we are participating in Christ's redeeming love. We are extending His mercy across the threshold of time and eternity.

In today's Gospel, the Lord promises: "This is the will of my Father, that I should not lose anything of what He gave me, but that I should raise it on the last day." (John 6:39). Here lies the foundation of our hope. The mercy of Christ is patient, purifying, and perfecting. The Redeemer who died for us does not abandon His own in death; He brings them through death to Himself. The souls in Purgatory are not forgotten; they are beloved, sustained by our prayers, and secure in divine promise.

Heaven is the vision of God "face to face" (1 Corinthians 13:12)—the fulfillment of every longing of the human heart. Hell is the eternal isolation of the self that refuses love. But Purgatory is the threshold of heaven, the antechamber of glory, the place where divine justice and mercy meet in the fire of love.

Today the Church invites us to pray, to intercede, and to hope. Remember the dead—not in sorrow, but in communion. Offer the Holy Sacrifice of the Mass for them. Live in the awareness that our lives, too, are moving toward eternity. The saints in heaven rejoice for us; the souls in Purgatory depend upon us.

This day is not one of despair, but of luminous realism and supernatural hope. It reminds us that God is both just and merciful;

that death is real, but so is resurrection; that we must never presume upon grace, but always trust in it.

Let us entrust our beloved dead to the mercy of God, and let us purify our own hearts so that, when our hour comes, we may be ready to see Him face to face.

"Eternal rest grant unto them, O Lord, and let perpetual light shine upon them. May they rest in peace. Amen."

Second Sunday in Ordinary Time

We stand at the threshold of Ordinary Time, yet what we behold today is anything but ordinary. Saint John the Baptist speaks the words that the Church echoes at every Mass: "Behold the Lamb of God." In this profound moment, the Baptist identifies Jesus not merely by His name or lineage, but by His mission: He is the Lamb who takes away the sin of the world.

To understand the weight of John's declaration, we must recall the Old Testament context. The Passover lamb (Exodus 12), whose blood saved Israel from death and slavery, becomes the typological foundation for the identity of Christ. The Prophet Isaiah, in today's first reading, speaks of a Servant whose mission is to be a light to the nations and to bring salvation to the ends of the earth (Isaiah 49:6).

In the figure of Christ, these threads converge. He is the new Isaac, the true Paschal Lamb, the Suffering Servant. As the Catechism of the Catholic Church teaches: "Christ's whole life is a mystery of redemption. Redemption comes to us above all through the blood of His cross, but this mystery is at work throughout Christ's entire life..." (*CCC* §517)

Thus, when John says, "Behold the Lamb of God," he is proclaiming the beginning of the new Exodus, the new creation.

St. Thomas Aquinas, in his *Commentary on the Gospel of John*, observes that John the Baptist did not say "the sins," plural, but "the sin," singular, of the world. Aquinas teaches that this reveals the universality of sin and the totality of Christ's redemptive mission. The Lamb does not merely atone for individual failings, but for the very condition of alienation and brokenness introduced by original sin.

"He did not say, 'who takes away the sins of the world,' but 'the sin,' that is, the whole mass and body of sin, or the root of sin, namely, original sin." (*Super Ioan., c. 1, l. 10*)

This is not mere forgiveness; it is ontological healing. Christ takes upon Himself the weight of sin so that we might be restored to communion with the Father.

Christ is not only the one who removes sin, but the revelation of divine love in its most radical form. Christ's identity is mission: the Son exists to be sent, to give Himself.

When John the Baptist says, "I did not know him," it is not a statement of ignorance, but of revelation. Christ can only be recognized when He appears in the form of the Lamb, the one who comes not in dominion but in self-offering. The Trinity is revealed not in glory alone, but in the kenosis of the Son—a humility that radiates divine love.

John testifies: "I saw the Spirit come down like a dove from heaven and remain upon him." This marks not only Christ's identity but the inauguration of His public ministry. The "remaining" of the Spirit points to the permanent anointing of Jesus as the Christos, the Anointed One, fulfilling Isaiah 61:1: *"The Spirit of the Lord is upon me, for He has anointed me."*

According to the Fathers of the Church, particularly St. Cyril of Jerusalem, this descent of the Spirit is not for Christ's sake—who is already one with the Spirit from eternity—but for ours: "The Holy Spirit came down upon Him in bodily form not for His sake, but for ours, so that we might know that the Spirit rests upon Him." (*Catechetical Lectures*, 17.9)

St. Paul reminds us in the second reading that we are "called to be holy." The Lamb who takes away sin does not merely leave us cleansed—He leaves us commissioned. To "behold the Lamb" is to follow the Lamb wherever He goes (Revelation 14:4). It is to take up the cross, to share in His mission of love and reconciliation.

As we receive the Eucharist, we hear those same words: "Behold the Lamb of God..." It is a summons not to passive piety but to active discipleship. The Lamb we behold is the Lamb we receive. And the Lamb we receive is the Lamb we must become: offering ourselves in love to the world.

As we begin this liturgical season of "ordinary" time, let us remember that nothing is ordinary after the Incarnation. The Lamb of God walks among us. He takes away our sin. He calls us to holiness. Let us behold Him, follow Him, and become one with Him—so that, in us, the world may see not just a teacher, not merely a prophet, but the Lamb who was slain and lives forever.

Third Sunday in Ordinary Time

This Sunday, we are drawn into the luminous clarity of Christ's mission. We are given to behold the light that breaks upon the land of Zebulun and Naphtali, a land once engulfed in darkness. With these words, the prophet Isaiah prefigures the arrival of the Messiah, and St. Matthew makes it clear: Jesus is the fulfillment of this prophecy.

In the first reading, Isaiah speaks into a situation of national despair—the devastation of the northern territories during the Assyrian conquest. Yet he promises: *"The people who walked in darkness have seen a great light."* This is not simply poetic hope; it is a prophetic foretelling. Christ is that light, and His public ministry begins in precisely those same territories. In this, geography becomes theology: the Messiah begins His ministry in the margins, to reveal that salvation comes not from the center of power but from the peripheries.

As the Catechism states: "Jesus is the light of the world, the light of men who shines in the darkness and enlightens every man." (*CCC¥541*)

To encounter Christ is to undergo a paschal illumination. Where He walks, the darkness flees.

St. Paul's words to the Corinthians strike a different chord: *"Let there be no divisions among you."* The Apostle pleads for unity, which flows not from human consensus but from shared participation in Christ crucified. As St. Thomas Aquinas notes in his *Commentary on 1 Corinthians*, "Christ is not divided, nor should the faithful be divided, since they are one body in Him."

Division in the Church, for Aquinas, is not merely a practical concern but a theological wound to the Body of Christ. Unity is not uniformity, but a participation in the same source: the cross and the sacraments. To walk in the light is to walk with one another, joined not by ideology but by the blood of Christ.

Matthew tells us that Jesus begins His preaching with the words: *"Repent, for the kingdom of heaven is at hand."* Immediately He calls Simon Peter and Andrew, then James and John.

Peter and Andrew are not called because they are extraordinary; they are called because Christ chooses them. His call makes them extraordinary. And so it is with each of us: vocation is not a personal project, but a divine gift. When Christ calls, He does not simply invite; He creates.

Christ does not merely gather disciples; He forms a communion. His ministry is not solo; it is always relational. As St. John Chrysostom preaches: "Christ calls them two by two to show that no one should journey alone, but that discipleship is a shared path." (*Homilies on Matthew*)

This shared discipleship becomes the seed of the Church. The same Christ who walked by the Sea of Galilee walks now into our lives. He speaks the same words: *"Follow me."* And to follow Him means to leave behind the boats and the nets—whatever binds us to darkness—and to enter into the work of light.

The Church, founded upon these first called disciples, continues the mission of light. The Catechism beautifully declares: "The Church is in history, but she transcends it. It is only with the eyes of faith that one can see her in her visible reality and at the same time in her spiritual reality as bearer of divine life." (*CCC* 770)

Thus, to be the Church is to be missionary. Not all are called to leave their boats in the same way, but all are called to participate in Christ's light. Our task is not to manufacture the light, but to reflect it faithfully.

Today, Christ walks by the shores of our lives. He sees us, knows us, calls us. The darkness has not disappeared, but the light shines in the darkness, and the darkness has not overcome it (John 1:5).

So let us go, leaving behind division, fear, and comfort. Let us walk together in unity and mission. Let us, like those first disciples, follow the Lamb who is our Light. For where He walks, heaven draws near.

Fourth Sunday in Ordinary Time

Today we hear the beginning of the greatest sermon ever preached: the Sermon on the Mount, a summit of Gospel revelation that begins with paradox: "Blessed are the poor, the mournful, the meek..." With these words, Jesus opens the path to beatitude, turning upside down every worldly expectation of power, prestige, and comfort.

St. Augustine calls the Beatitudes "a perfect number of Christian virtues", each corresponding to the journey of the soul toward God. But more than moral instructions, the Beatitudes are first and foremost a portrait of Christ Himself.

Christ does not simply teach the Beatitudes; He is the Beatitude. To be poor in spirit, to hunger for righteousness, to suffer persecution—this is Christ's life, and by grace, it becomes ours.

In his Summa Theologiae (*I-II, q. 3*), St. Thomas Aquinas explores the question: *What is happiness?* He concludes that true beatitudo cannot be found in wealth, pleasure, fame, or power—all are finite. True happiness is found only in the vision of God.

The Beatitudes, then, are paradoxical paths that dispose us to receive this divine life. Aquinas writes: "The Beatitudes are the acts of the virtues perfected by the gifts of the Holy Spirit, which lead to the ultimate end: the enjoyment of God." (*ST* I-II, q. 69, a.1)

Thus, poverty of spirit is not a rejection of the world, but a humble receptivity to God. Mourning is not despair, but a longing for redemption. The Beatitudes do not diminish human life—they elevate it to divine communion.

Christ's glory is revealed not in triumph but in kenosis — self-emptying love. The Beatitudes are not a spiritual strategy but an invitation into the form of Christ:

The world recoils from meekness and suffering, but the Cross reveals them as the true grammar of divine love. In the Beatitudes, Christ offers us not a new law, but His own form, which the saints have embodied throughout history.

The Fathers of the Church saw the Beatitudes as a ladder of ascent. St. Gregory of Nyssa compares them to Moses ascending Mount Sinai: "Each beatitude is a step, lifting the soul to a greater likeness of God."

And St. John Chrysostom emphasizes the radical nature of this teaching: "Jesus begins His preaching with blessings for the very things the world despises. He reveals a kingdom of inversion, where humility reigns, and purity is crowned."

The Beatitudes are the new commandments of the new Moses, spoken not from a mountain of stone, but from the mountain of mercy.

Today's reading from Zephaniah speaks of a "humble and lowly remnant" who will take refuge in the Lord. The Church, in every age, is called to be this anawim, the "little flock" (Luke 12:32) whose strength lies not in human glory but in divine fidelity. St. Paul in the second reading reminds us that God chooses the weak to shame the strong.

The Church must always be poor in spirit—not self-reliant but God-reliant. The Beatitudes must shape our witness in the world: not as triumphalism, but as cruciform hope.

The Greek word for "blessed" in the Beatitudes is *makarios*, which denotes a deep spiritual joy flowing from communion with God. The Beatitudes, then, are not merely ethical teachings; they are an invitation to share in the interior life of Christ.

To live the Beatitudes is to be shaped by the Cross and illumined by the Resurrection. It is to be prepared for the only true happiness: the vision of God, the end for which we were made.

Let us ask the Lord today for the grace not merely to admire the Beatitudes, but to embody them. For only in this way do we become salt of the earth and light of the world (cf. Matthew 5:13-14).

Fifth Sunday in Ordinary Time

Last Sunday, we stood on the Mount with Jesus as He proclaimed the Beatitudes—the blueprint for the Christian life. Today, the Lord tells us what happens when that life is actually lived: the world is seasoned and illuminated. Christ proclaims: "You are the salt of the earth. You are the light of the world."

Salt and light are not optional spiritual add-ons. They are intrinsic to Christian identity. As St. John Chrysostom observes: "He did not say, 'You must become salt and light,' but 'You are' — for in baptism and faith, you are already commissioned with this mission." (*Homilies on Matthew*)

Salt preserves, flavors, and purifies. In the ancient world, it was essential for sustaining life. Light reveals, directs, and dispels darkness. To be salt and light is to embody the presence of Christ in the world: to preserve truth, reveal goodness, and shine with divine beauty.

This calling flows not from self-promotion, but from participation in Christ. As the Catechism of the Catholic Church teaches: "The baptized, by virtue of their baptism, share in the priesthood of Christ, in his prophetic and royal mission." (*CCC* §854)

In his Commentary on the Gospel of Matthew, St. Thomas Aquinas explains that when Jesus speaks of good works shining before others, He does not mean a display for vanity but for edification: "Let your light shine, not that you may be praised, but that God may be glorified in you." (*Super Matt., c. 5, l. 3*)

Our works must be visible not as personal achievements but as signs of grace at work. The Christian does not shine with a borrowed glow, but with the indwelling light of Christ.

Furthermore, Aquinas teaches that charity is the form of all virtue. Without it, even acts of external piety are empty. Thus, Isaiah's prophecy in today's first reading becomes a foundation: *"Share your bread with the hungry... then your light shall break forth like the dawn."* (Isaiah 58:7-10)

The Church must be the form of Christ in the world. Christian mission is not primarily activism, but visibility of divine love. The world does not need more rhetoric; it needs witnesses. The Church shines when she offers not slogans but sanctity.

St. Paul, in today's second reading, speaks of his mission in Corinth with fear and trembling. He did not come with persuasive speech but in the power of the Spirit. Why?

Because true evangelization is not manipulation, but manifestation. God does not require eloquence; He desires openness. As Augustine says: "Do not think that you make the gospel powerful. Rather, it is the gospel that makes you powerful." (*Sermon 229E*). Paul's poverty of speech allows the power of Christ to shine more clearly.

In this brief but potent Gospel, Christ reminds us: our lives must be luminous. But how?

- Through acts of mercy: feeding, clothing, comforting.
- Through fidelity in suffering: trusting in the Lord amid trial.
- Through joy in daily life: a joy not of circumstance, but of communion with God.

In a culture allergic to truth and allergic to suffering, the luminous life of the Christian becomes a contradiction and a revelation. We must never retreat into private religiosity, for Christ says: *"A city set on a hill cannot be hidden."*

Salt that loses its taste is good for nothing. Light hidden under a bushel is wasted. Christ has made us salt and light by grace. We are called to season the world with truth and illuminate it with love.

So let us shine—not with our own brilliance, but with the radiance of Christ. Let our lives speak of His mercy, our actions point to His truth, and our presence become sacramental in the world: a visible sign of the invisible kingdom.

Sixth Sunday in Ordinary Time

Today's Gospel plunges us into the heart of Jesus' teaching in the Sermon on the Mount. Far from relaxing the commandments of the Old Law, Christ reveals their inner truth, their fullest expression, their perfection in charity. As the Church Fathers consistently taught, Christ is not the destroyer of the Law, but its divine interpreter and fulfillment.

The Book of Sirach reminds us that God has placed before us life and death, good and evil, and has granted us the freedom to choose. This is not Pelagian self-sufficiency, but a truth echoed in the Catechism of the Catholic Church: "Freedom is the power, rooted in reason and will, to act or not to act... to perform deliberate actions on one's own responsibility." (*CCC* §1733)

In the Gospel, Jesus radicalizes the Law by internalizing it: not only must we avoid murder, we must purge anger; not only must we avoid adultery, we must purify our gaze; not only must we speak the truth, we must be transparent in all speech.

This is the law of the New Covenant: not one written on stone, but written in the heart by the Holy Spirit (cf. Jer 31:33).

St. Thomas Aquinas, in the *Summa Theologiae*, explores the perfection of the New Law. He explains that the Old Law restrained sin externally, but the New Law gives grace to transform the heart: "The New Law is chiefly the grace of the Holy Spirit, given through faith in Christ." (*ST* I-II, q. 106, a.1)

For Aquinas, the moral precepts of the Old Law are not abolished but fulfilled interiorly, elevated and perfected by grace. Christ's words in Matthew 5 are not new moralism; they are graced realism. The commandments are not burdens, but signposts to beatitude when animated by love.

True morality is never abstract. It is always Christological. Jesus does not present an ethic, but a form of life to which to be conformed. The Beatitudes, and today's challenging Gospel, are not mere standards to meet; they are participations in the very life of Christ. He does not just command; He forms us into His likeness. This is not about sin management. It is about transformation by divine love.

St. Augustine reads today's Gospel as Christ's way of healing the root of sin: "The law was given that grace might be sought; grace was given that the law might be fulfilled." (*De Spiritu et Littera*, 19.33)

Christ addresses not only actions, but desires. He offers not merely pardon, but healing of the heart. Likewise, Origen teaches that Jesus, the Logos, brings not a higher legalism but a deeper purification of the soul, so that we may become "luminous like the angels."

St. Paul tells us in today's second reading that the wisdom of God is hidden from the rulers of this age. It is not cleverness or calculation; it is cruciform wisdom. What Christ proposes in the Sermon on the Mount can only be lived by those who have received the Spirit (cf. 1 Cor 2:10), who can discern "the depths of God." This is not a burden for the elite, but a call to deep intimacy with the crucified and risen Lord.

Jesus calls us today not to mere exterior compliance but to interior transformation. He wants our hearts, our thoughts, our intentions. He wants to make us holy from the inside out.

Let us beg the Holy Spirit to write His law anew on our hearts, to make us truthful, pure, merciful, and peaceable. In a world of duplicity, vengeance, and lust, let us be men and women of the Beatitudes—formed by the Word, sustained by the Sacraments, and conformed to Christ. For He alone is the true fulfillment of the Law.

Seventh Sunday in Ordinary Time

Today's Gospel confronts us with one of the most demanding and luminous commands of the entire Christian life: *"Love your enemies"* and *"Be perfect, as your heavenly Father is perfect."* This is not poetic exaggeration, nor an unattainable moral ideal. It is the revelation of divine charity—the very heart of Christian holiness.

The first reading from Leviticus sets the pattern: *"You shall be holy, for I the Lord your God am holy"* (Leviticus 19:2). Holiness for Israel meant consecration—being set apart for God, purified from idolatry, and shaped by covenant fidelity. But in Christ, holiness is transfigured: it is no longer separation from others, but transformation into love for all, even for one's enemies.

St. John Chrysostom, in his *Homilies on Matthew*, reminds us: "To love those who love us is mere natural affection; to love our enemies is divine." (Homily 18 on Matthew 5:46–47)

This is not sentimentality but participation in God's own mode of being. For to love one's enemies is to share in that same love by which God "makes his sun rise on the evil and on the good, and sends rain on the just and on the unjust" (Matthew 5:45). It is to let divine grace expand the narrow borders of the human heart.

St. Thomas Aquinas, in the *Summa Theologiae*, teaches that "the perfection of the Christian life consists chiefly in charity" (*ST* II-II, q.184, a.1, *respondeo*). Commenting on this same passage of Matthew, he explains: "The perfection which Christ calls for consists in the love of God and neighbor, extended even to enemies, which is the greatest sign of the divine image in man." (*Catena Aurea* on Matthew 5:48)

Aquinas insists that Christ does not abolish the Law of Moses but brings it to its completion: the moral precepts find their fulfillment in the perfection of love. To love one's enemies is to reflect the Creator's own nature, for divine love is diffusive of itself, pouring out even upon those who reject it.

This perfection is not moral self-improvement or sinless flawlessness; it is communion in the divine life. As St. Paul declares, *"The love of God has been poured into our hearts through the Holy Spirit who has been given to us"* (Romans 5:5). We are temples of this indwelling love: *"Do you not know that you are the temple of God, and that the Spirit of God dwells in you?"* (1 Corinthians 3:16).

The *Catechism of the Catholic Church* echoes this mystery: "By loving even our enemies, we become children of our Father in heaven." (CCC 1825)

The perfection that Jesus commands is, therefore, not static moral completeness but the maturation of charity. St. Gregory of Nyssa describes this sanctifying dynamism beautifully: "He who ascends never stops going from beginning to beginning, through beginnings that never end." (*Homily on the Song of Songs*, II)

Perfection, then, is an ever-deepening participation in the infinite love of God. Holiness is growth without limit, movement without rest, because the One we love is without limit and without end.

Origen, in his *Commentary on Matthew*, saw in the love of enemies the highest imitation of God, for "he who loves those who hate him becomes most like to God, who loved even those who sinned against Him." Love of enemies is therefore not natural virtue but supernatural likeness—it is to live *in Deo*, in God Himself.

St. Augustine brings this reflection to its radiant simplicity when he says: "The measure of love is to love without measure." (*De Catechizandis Rudibus*, 4.8)

To love without measure is to let divine charity overflow every boundary—resentment, rivalry, pride, or fear. It is to let the Cross interpret love. For on the Cross, Christ loved those who crucified Him; He prayed for His enemies, blessed those who cursed Him, and forgave those who struck Him. There, love becomes cruciform—self-emptying, kenotic, victorious. Christ is not merely an example to imitate but the form into which grace conforms us.

This love is not achieved by human strength. It is gift before it is command. What seems impossible to man is possible for God (cf. Luke 18:27). Christ does not merely tell us to love this way—He gives us His Spirit to make it possible. In the Eucharist, the Sacrament of Love, we are nourished by that same charity which we are commanded to live. Each reception of Holy Communion deepens our capacity to love as we have been loved.

Forgiveness, generosity, and patience are the lived texture of divine life within us. Forgiveness is not only letting go of resentment, but blessing those who curse us. Generosity is not calculating fairness, but giving beyond what is required. Patience is enduring wrongs without retaliation, bearing the cross of another's weakness in love. These are not optional virtues; they are the concrete signs that divine charity is at work in us.

To love our enemies and to be perfect as the Father is perfect seems humanly unattainable. And it is—apart from grace. But grace is never absent from those who seek it. The perfection Christ commands is the perfection He Himself imparts. As Chrysostom wrote in another homily, "When you see someone loving his enemies, remember that this is the work of God's grace."

Let us go forth, then, not in fear of our weakness, but in the hope of His strength. For in Christ, divine perfection has been revealed; through Him, it can be lived. And when we love without measure, we bear the unmistakable resemblance of children to their Father in heaven.

Eighth Sunday in Ordinary Time

"In today's Gospel, Our Lord speaks with a kind of serene authority that both comforts and confronts: "Do not worry about your life… but seek first the Kingdom of God."

This is not the language of detachment born of apathy. It is not Stoic denial of emotion. It is the voice of the Divine Word who knows the human heart. Christ does not deny the reality of our concerns — He reorders them. His command not to worry is not a prohibition but an invitation: to step out of the narrow confines of self-preoccupation and to entrust ourselves entirely to the Father's providential care.

St. Augustine, who knew restlessness intimately, reads this Gospel as a summons to reorient desire itself. He writes in *On Christian Doctrine*: "For to enjoy a thing is to rest with satisfaction in it for its own sake. To use, on the other hand, is to employ whatever means are at one's disposal to obtain what one desires." (I.4.4)

And later, he summarizes the entire movement of the spiritual life: "God alone to be enjoyed." (I.22)

The problem, Augustine insists, is not the possession of things but the possession of the soul by things. Anxiety grows where attachment tightens. When we live as if our identity depends upon the world's provision, we become enslaved to contingency. To "seek first the Kingdom" is to allow God to reorder the hierarchy of our loves — to move from worry (*cura*) to charity (*caritas*). Detachment, for Augustine, is not cold renunciation but burning love rightly directed. The human heart is not made to be emptied but to be filled — not with mammon, but with God Himself.

The first reading gives the tender image of Divine Providence: "Can a mother forget her infant?... Even should she forget, I will never forget you." (Isaiah 49:15)

Providence, St. Thomas Aquinas teaches, is "the type of the order of things towards an end pre-existing in the divine mind" (*ST* I, q.22, a.1). In other words, it is the eternal wisdom of God applied to the details of creation. Aquinas, following Boethius, calls providence "the divine type itself, seated in the Supreme Ruler, which disposeth all things." This providence is not abstract fate but the wise ordering of divine love. It does not mean exemption from suffering, but rather purpose within suffering. It is through the cruciform pattern of life — through limitation, failure, and even sorrow — that God's design draws the soul toward its true good.

Aquinas also clarifies that not all concern for temporal things is forbidden. He writes, "Not all solicitude about temporal things is forbidden, but that which is superfluous and inordinate" (*ST* II-II, q.83, a.6, ad 2*). It is lawful, he says, "to desire temporal things, not indeed principally... but as helps whereby we are assisted in tending towards beatitude" (*ibid., respondeo*). Christ, then, does not forbid labor or prudence, but the anxious care that springs from lack of faith. We are called to work, but not to worry; to act prudently, but not to be consumed by the illusion that we control the outcome.

Why does Christ insist that "you cannot serve both God and mammon"? Because anxiety, at its root, is a symptom of divided allegiance. The anxious heart seeks control in order to secure its own happiness. But the will that clings to control cannot receive grace. The soul at peace is not one free from problems, but one whose will has been surrendered to the Divine Will. Prayer is the school of holy abandonment. In true prayer, the will is stretched beyond the narrow circle of the self and begins to breathe in the rhythm of divine trust.

This freedom is what St. Paul calls "the freedom of the children of God" (Romans 8:21). It is not autonomy, but filial confidence — the serene assurance that the Father's care extends even to "the hairs of your head."

In the second reading, Paul reminds the Corinthians that he and his companions are "stewards of the mysteries of God." A steward does not own; he administers what belongs to Another. The Christian life is precisely this: to recognize that everything — our talents, our time, even our trials — are entrusted, not possessed. Paul then adds a line that should disarm every anxious heart: "It is the Lord who judges me." How much energy we expend trying to justify ourselves — to others, to the world, even to our own inner critic. But Paul's peace comes from knowing that his worth is not measured by appearances or outcomes. He lives under the gaze of the Father, whose judgment is mercy. The mature Christian, like Paul, is free from the tyranny of human approval because his heart rests in divine affirmation.

St. John Chrysostom captures the heart of this Gospel with paternal simplicity: "Let us not therefore be anxious, for we shall gain nothing by it, but tormenting ourselves." (*Homilies on Matthew*, 22)

And elsewhere he adds: "Seek the things in Heaven... therefore He does all to deliver us from things unnecessary, and from our affection for the earth." (*Homilies on Matthew*, 22)

Anxiety thrives in the imagined future. Grace, however, is always in the present. To live by faith is to live in what the spiritual tradition calls *the sacrament of the present moment* — to find, here and now, the fidelity of God. The *Catechism of the Catholic Church* reminds us: "Our Father knows what we need before we ask him… We must pray, then, with his Spirit of freedom, to be able truly to know what he wants." (CCC 2736)

When we seek first the Kingdom, we cease grasping for control over tomorrow and instead discover the hidden abundance of today. Divine grace is never theoretical — it is incarnate, timely, and sufficient.

To "seek first the Kingdom" is not a slogan but a program of conversion. It calls for a radical reorientation of life — that Christ may become the measure of all choices, the origin of all action, and the end of all desire. To seek the Kingdom is to believe that God's will is more loving than our own plans. It is to let our anxieties become occasions for surrender. It is to discover that trust is not naivety but courage — the courage to rest in the Father's love when everything else seems uncertain.

Let us examine our hearts: Where does mammon still rule? What do I fear more than I trust? What do I cling to that prevents me from resting in the Father's providence?

The one who trusts in God is not free from trials, but is free *within* them. For the believer, serenity is not the absence of storms but the presence of Christ within the boat. Let us pray for the grace of holy detachment — that we may live as faithful stewards, trust as beloved children, and seek the Kingdom first, confident that all else will be given unto us.

Ninth Sunday in Ordinary Time

Today, the Lord draws the Sermon on the Mount to a dramatic conclusion. He warns us: it is not enough to hear the Word—we must live it. He invites us not merely to confess Him with our lips, but to conform our lives to His teaching. What we build our life upon matters.

In Deuteronomy, Moses urges the people of Israel to bind the Word of God to their hearts. Why? Because blessing or curse depends upon obedience or disobedience to the covenant. Jesus echoes this ancient covenant logic: to build on the rock is to live His Word.

St. Augustine explains: "Not the one who says 'Lord, Lord' but the one who does what the Lord commands builds on rock." (*Sermon 26.2*)

Faith is not a feeling or a mere assent of the intellect. It is the submission of the whole person to God. To build on Christ is to place Him at the center of every decision.

St. Thomas Aquinas, in his *Commentary on Matthew,* teaches that this Gospel refers to the distinction between faith that is living and faith that is dead. He writes: "To build on rock is to have faith formed by charity. It is not enough to believe; one must love." For Aquinas, the one who merely hears is like someone who possesses knowledge without allowing it to shape his life. But faith that is formed by love bears fruit in obedience.

The form of Christ is not an idea to be admired but a life to be conformed to. The Sermon on the Mount is not idealistic moralism; it is the form of the Son given for our imitation. To build on Christ is to allow our lives to be structured by His cross, not by comfort, popularity, or personal advantage. The storms come for all. Only the house founded on Christ will stand.

In Romans, St. Paul proclaims that righteousness comes not from works of the Law, but through faith in Jesus Christ. But this faith is not passive. It is the gift of participation in Christ's own obedience: "This faith is active in love, rooted in grace, and aimed toward glory." (*cf. Rom 3:24-25*)

Faith is the doorway to divine life, and the Sermon on the Mount is its blueprint. Without this living structure of holiness, our house remains exposed to collapse.

Origen sees in the wise builder a model of the ascetic and contemplative life: "The one who builds on rock not only listens with reverence, but also practices virtue and stands firm under trial."

Likewise, St. Gregory the Great comments: "There are some who hear the Word of God and receive it with joy, yet they lack the root of endurance and fall when adversity comes."

The Fathers warn us that orthodoxy without orthopraxy is insufficient. The house must not only be adorned with beautiful creeds but anchored in faithful deeds.

We live in a time of storm: cultural upheaval, moral confusion, spiritual apathy. The rain falls. The rivers rise. The winds blow. What will hold?

Only the house built on Christ.

Let us ask the Lord today: What is the foundation of my life? Am I building on the solid rock, or on shifting sands? Do I merely profess faith, or do I embody it?

May the Word we hear at this Mass become the foundation of our lives. May Christ dwell in our hearts through faith (cf. Eph 3:17), and may our lives reflect the truth we profess.

Tenth Sunday in Ordinary Time

In today's Gospel, Christ calls Matthew from his tax booth and says, "Follow me." In this simple yet transformative encounter, we see the essence of divine mercy. The one who seemed disqualified becomes a disciple. The sinner becomes an apostle. Mercy is not merely God's *feeling* toward sinners; it is His *mission*.

Our first reading from Hosea gives us the interpretive key to the Gospel. God says, "It is love that I desire, not sacrifice; knowledge of God rather than burnt offerings." The Hebrew word for love here is *hesed* — steadfast, covenantal mercy. Hosea speaks to a people going through the motions of religion while their hearts are far from the Lord. The prophet reminds us: external ritual without interior conversion is hollow.

St. John Chrysostom warns: "God does not reject sacrifice, but sacrifice offered without a merciful heart."

In the *Summa Theologiae* (*ST* I, q. 21, a. 3), St. Thomas Aquinas teaches that "mercy is the greatest of the divine attributes in its effects" because it presupposes justice but goes beyond it. God's mercy is not injustice but a superabundance of goodness, healing, and transformation.

Commenting on today's Gospel, Aquinas writes: "Christ chose sinners not because they were righteous, but that through Him they might become righteous." Thus, Matthew's call is a sign that grace precedes merit. Christ does not wait for us to be worthy; He makes us worthy by His call. The beauty of Christ's form is revealed most strikingly in His gaze of love upon sinners.

In the second reading, St. Paul speaks of Abraham's faith: *"He believed, hoping against hope."* This same faith undergirds Matthew's response to Jesus. The apostolic life begins not with perfection but with trust. As with Abraham, faith is reckoned as righteousness (Rom 4:22).

Abraham and Matthew both act on a divine initiative. The human response to grace is to trust that God's call can overcome our past and empower our future.

The Catechism of the Catholic Church affirms: "Jesus invites sinners to the table of the Kingdom: 'Come to me, all who labor and are heavy laden.' He calls them to conversion and, by showing them in word and deed His Father's boundless mercy, draws them into the fold of God" (*CCC* §1425).

This is not cheap grace. It is mercy that calls to conversion, to a life no longer built on self but on Christ.

Origen calls Christ the true Physician of souls: "He does not heal from afar, but enters the house of the sinner."

And St. Gregory the Great writes: "He who calls Matthew the tax collector takes no account of what he was but considers what he will become."

This is the logic of divine mercy: it sees the end from the beginning, not as fate, but as vocation.

Christ's gaze falls upon each of us today. We, too, are Matthews—not because we collect taxes, but because we all sit at booths of self-interest and sin. But Jesus says to us: "Follow me."

Will we rise? Will we leave behind the table of our false securities?

Let us go to the altar today like Matthew went to dinner with Christ: not because we are worthy, but because we are called. And let us live as people transformed by mercy, seeking not sacrifice alone, but love, steadfast and true.

Eleventh Sunday in Ordinary Time

In today's Gospel, we see the very heart of Christ's mission revealed in one word: *splagchnizomai*—"He was moved with compassion." This is not a mere feeling of pity; it is a deep, visceral movement of divine love, a love that refuses to remain distant from human misery. Saint Thomas Aquinas describes mercy (*misericordia*) as "a kind of sorrow for another's distress, as though it were one's own" (*STh* II–II, q.30, a.1). In Christ, this is not metaphor but mystery: the Eternal Word takes our weakness upon Himself. His divine heart beats with human compassion.

Christ's compassion, then, is not sentimentality; it is salvific. It leads Him to act. Seeing the lost and weary crowds, "like sheep without a shepherd," He calls the Twelve—not merely to admire His compassion, but to share in it. "He summoned His twelve disciples and gave them authority" (Mt 10:1). Here, mission flows directly from communion. Christ calls, names, and sends. The same movement continues in the Church: the one who is called must be sent.

Aquinas helps us understand this dynamic of vocation and mission through his teaching on grace and charity. "The love of charity," he writes, "moves us to desire and work for the good of others" (*STh* II–II, q.23, a.1). The compassion of Christ, then, is not only His emotion—it becomes the form of our mission, the interior principle that propels the apostolic life. When we love with Christ's charity, we are drawn into His own redemptive purpose.

The first reading from Exodus reminds us that Israel's election is not for privilege but for service: "You shall be to me a kingdom of priests and a holy nation." Aquinas notes that priesthood is defined by mediation—"it belongs to a priest to stand between the people and God, and to offer up the people's prayers to God and the divine gifts to the people" (*STh* III, q.22, a.1). The Church, as the new People of God, shares in this mediatorial role through baptism. Every Christian participates, in some measure, in Christ's priestly compassion—bearing others before the Lord in prayer and bringing the Lord's mercy to others in action.

To be a disciple, then, is to be both contemplative and apostolic. Aquinas writes that "the contemplative life precedes and causes the active life" (*STh* II–II, q.182, a.1). Before the Twelve are sent, they are first gathered. Before they proclaim, they are taught. Mission begins not with strategy but with contemplation—with allowing ourselves to be seen and loved by Christ. From that gaze, all authentic apostolic energy flows.

Saint Paul reminds us in Romans that "while we were still sinners, Christ died for us." Aquinas comments that "Christ died out of charity, and therefore His Passion was more pleasing to God than all the sacrifices of the Old Law" (*STh* III, q.48, a.2). The Cross is thus the supreme act of mercy—God's compassion translated into action. And it is from this fountain that every mission of the Church draws its life.

We are not called because we are righteous, but precisely because we are loved. "The reason of the Divine love is found in God, not in us" (*STh* I, q.20, a.2). This truth preserves us from both pride and despair: pride, because we recognize that the call is pure gift; despair, because that gift does not depend on our perfection but on God's generosity.

The Catechism reminds us that Christ "took our infirmities and bore our diseases" (CCC §1505). In this light, the Church is not an escape from the world's pain but a healing presence within it—a "field hospital," as Pope Francis loves to say. Aquinas anticipates this image when he writes that "mercy is the greatest of the virtues that relate to our neighbor" (*STh*II–II, q.30, a.4). To show mercy is to imitate God most perfectly, for "it belongs to God to have mercy, and therein His omnipotence is chiefly manifested" (*STh* II–II, q.30, a.4, ad 1).

The apostles are sent, therefore, not as judges but as healers—sent to cleanse, restore, and proclaim. Their authority is not domination but participation in Christ's compassionate power. The same holds true for us: our vocation is not to condemn the world, but to reveal within it the saving tenderness of God.

Finally, Christ tells us: "The harvest is abundant, but the laborers are few." Aquinas observes that "the end of charity is the love of God, but its effect is the love of neighbor" (*STh* II–II, q.25, a.1). To labor in the harvest is to let that charity take flesh in works of mercy, evangelization, and witness. The harvest belongs to the Lord, but the laborers are His instruments—hearts set aflame by divine compassion.

Let us, then, be renewed by the gaze of Christ that called the Twelve. Let His compassion move us, as it moved Him. Let us go forth as laborers in His vineyard—priests of mercy, ambassadors of reconciliation, heralds of the Kingdom where Love Himself reigns.

Twelfth Sunday in Ordinary Time

Fear stalks both Jeremiah and the apostles. The prophet laments, "Terror on every side!" (Jer 20:10). Betrayal closes in; even his friends conspire against him. Likewise, in today's Gospel, Jesus prepares His disciples for persecution, rejection, and misunderstanding. Yet three times He commands them: *"Do not be afraid."*

Why? Because faith reveals a reality deeper than fear: we are not forgotten by God. Christ tells us that not even a sparrow falls to the ground apart from the Father's will. The smallest detail of creation, the most fleeting moment of suffering—nothing escapes the providential gaze of God. As St. Thomas Aquinas teaches, "All things are subject to divine providence, not only in general, but even in their every detail" (*STh* I, q.22, a.2).

To be known by God, then, is not simply to be observed, but to be lovingly held in existence at every moment. "The very being of things," Aquinas writes, "depends upon God's providence, as the effect depends upon its cause" (*STh* I, q.22, a.3). Nothing—no threat, no betrayal, no suffering—can remove us from the sustaining care of the Father.

Yet fear persists in the human heart, because we are weak and wounded by sin. Into this weakness Christ descends. "While we were still sinners, Christ died for us," says St. Paul. Aquinas comments that "the Passion of Christ was the most perfect cause of our reconciliation with God" (*STh* III, q.49, a.1). The Cross transforms fear at its root, because in the Cross we see that even suffering and death have been overtaken by divine love.

Our courage as Christians, then, is not a stoic denial of danger but participation in the Redeemer's victory. Aquinas defines the virtue of fortitude as that which "strengthens the mind against fear of death" (*STh* II–II, q.123, a.4). It is not reckless daring, but "the firmness of soul in enduring evil for the sake of the good" (*STh* II–II, q.123, a.6). This virtue stands in the middle between cowardice and foolhardiness—it is a steady endurance born of faith in divine providence.

The fear that paralyzes us cannot be overcome by willpower alone. It yields only to charity—the love of God poured into our hearts by the Holy Spirit (Rom 5:5). "The perfection of charity casts out fear," Aquinas explains, "because fear regards a future evil, whereas charity unites us already to the highest good" (*STh* II–II, q.19, a.11).

Thus, the Christian who abides in charity is not untouched by anxiety, but is anchored beyond it. Love does not erase danger; it transforms it. The saints are courageous not because they are fearless, but because they are enflamed with divine charity. Their hearts are fixed where no enemy can reach—hidden, as Paul says, "with Christ in God" (Col 3:3).

This is why Aquinas teaches that "the love of God is the cause of all our good works" (*STh* II–II, q.27, a.8). Fortitude, then, is not self-generated heroism but the fruit of grace working through love. The more the soul clings to God, the less it is enslaved by fear.

Christ's final exhortation—"Do not be afraid of those who kill the body but cannot kill the soul"—reminds us that discipleship is public witness. To confess Christ before others is not optional; it is the overflow of interior conviction. Aquinas writes, "It is necessary for salvation to confess one's faith openly when silence would imply the denial of faith" (*STh* II–II, q.3, a.2).

This confession will often entail suffering. The disciple must be willing to share in the Cross. Yet even in persecution, there is peace. For "no created thing can separate us from the love of God" (*STh* I, q.20, a.3, ad 1).

To live in this confidence is to embody the serenity of Christ Himself—the One who stood before Pilate, silent yet sovereign. The saints are not anxious defenders of their own security, but radiant witnesses to the truth that God reigns even in suffering.

Jeremiah's cry of distress turns into a hymn of praise: "The Lord is with me like a mighty champion." Faith does not deny the storm; it trusts the One who commands it. Aquinas tells us that "to hope in God is to lean entirely upon His help" (*STh*II–II, q.17, a.5). This theological hope gives courage to endure whatever trials come, for it roots us in the certainty that God's providence is never absent.

And so, when Christ says, *"Do not be afraid,"* He is not offering comfort at a distance. He is revealing Himself as Emmanuel—God with us in every fear, every wound, every uncertainty. To trust this presence is to begin to taste the peace of the Kingdom even now.

Thirteenth Sunday in Ordinary Time

The paradox of the Gospel overturns our human instincts. We seek to preserve, to secure, to control. Yet Jesus proclaims: "Whoever finds his life will lose it, and whoever loses his life for My sake will find it." The Christian life begins not in grasping, but in surrender. In dying to self, we discover the freedom of divine love.

Aquinas captures this truth when he teaches that "the perfection of the Christian life consists in charity" (*STh* II–II, q.184, a.1). To live for Christ means to let charity—the love of God poured into our hearts by the Holy Spirit—become the form of all that we are and do. "Charity," he writes, "is the form of all the virtues, because it directs the acts of the other virtues to their ultimate end" (*STh* II–II, q.23, a.8). Every sacrifice, every act of service, every renunciation finds its meaning in love of God.

In the first reading, the Shunammite woman welcomes the prophet Elisha, providing him food, shelter, and rest. Her hospitality becomes the occasion of divine blessing. In her we see a figure of the soul who receives Christ. "To receive a prophet because he is a prophet," Jesus says, "will gain a prophet's reward."

Aquinas explains that the virtue of hospitality belongs to mercy, because "it relieves the needs of the stranger" (*STh* II–II, q.31, a.2). But when performed for the sake of Christ, it transcends mere human kindness—it becomes participation in divine charity. The guest becomes an image of God Himself. To welcome another in the name of Christ is to open the heart to grace. "Since charity unites us to God," Aquinas says, "it is through charity that we are made friends of God" (*STh* II–II, q.23, a.1).

Thus, the table of the Shunammite becomes a sanctuary, and the home a temple. The smallest gesture of love becomes the dwelling place of the divine.

Christ's words about taking up the cross are not a call to heroic suffering for its own sake, but an invitation to live according to the pattern of divine love. "To carry the cross," Aquinas notes, "is to submit to whatever burdens are laid upon us for the sake of God" (*STh* II–II, q.186, a.3). This is the daily martyrdom of discipleship—the offering of the self in ordinary fidelity, in hidden sacrifices, in the quiet perseverance of love.

Saint Paul tells us in Romans that through baptism we are "buried with Christ… so that we too might live in newness of life." Aquinas explains that "baptism is a configuration to Christ's death and resurrection" (*STh* III, q.66, a.7). The Christian, therefore, lives every day as one already raised from death. Our surrender does not end in loss; it flowers into participation in the risen life of Christ.

Jesus concludes today's Gospel with a tender image: "Whoever gives even a cup of cold water to one of these little ones because he is a disciple—amen, I say to you, he will surely not lose his reward." Divine reward is attached not to greatness, but to grace-filled simplicity. Aquinas reminds us that "charity does not measure the gift by its quantity, but by the affection with which it is given" (*STh* II–II, q.27, a.6). What matters is not the size of the act, but the love that animates it.

In this light, every act of mercy, every word of encouragement, every hidden sacrifice becomes radiant with eternal value. The smallest offering, made for love of Christ, participates in the infinite love by which He redeems the world.

The paradox of the Gospel—the way of losing to gain, dying to live—is not a contradiction but a revelation of divine wisdom. As Aquinas teaches, "The highest perfection of human life consists in this, that the human mind is united to God" (*STh* II–II, q.180, a.1). Union with God is the goal toward which every renunciation and every act of love is ordered.

The woman of Shunem opened her home; we are called to open our hearts. To love Christ above all is to love all things rightly. To take up the cross is to walk in freedom. To give a cup of cold water is to share in the generosity of God Himself.

This is the paradox that saves: in surrender, we find peace; in love, we find life everlasting.

Fourteenth Sunday in Ordinary Time

In a world that prizes power, speed, and visibility, today's Gospel unveils the quiet majesty of divine humility. Jesus, the Eternal Word made flesh, rejoices in the Father and proclaims: "I give you praise, Father, Lord of heaven and earth, for although you have hidden these things from the wise and learned, you have revealed them to the little ones."

This is not a glorification of ignorance, but of receptivity. The *nēpios*—the "infant" or "childlike" one—is not self-sufficient but dependent, not full but open. In such humility, divine wisdom finds a dwelling place. "God resists the proud but gives grace to the humble" (*STh* II–II, q.161, a.5, ad 1). Pride closes the soul to grace; humility opens it.

Aquinas defines humility as "keeping oneself within one's own bounds, not reaching out to things above one's capacity" (*STh* II–II, q.161, a.1). It is the disposition of a heart that knows it receives everything from God. For Aquinas, this humility is not servile or timid; it is luminous with truth. It allows the soul to rest—not in itself, but in the God who gives all.

Christ's words reveal a profound reversal. The Kingdom of God does not belong to the self-assured, but to those who know their dependence. The learned of this world may master concepts, but the childlike heart knows the Giver. "Wisdom enters into the humble and simple mind," writes Aquinas, "because such a one is ready to be taught by God" (*Commentary on Matthew*, 11:25).

This humility is not opposed to knowledge but to arrogance. It is the intellect purified by love. In this sense, every act of faith is an act of humility—the submission of the mind to divine truth. "By humility," Aquinas writes, "man submits himself to God, and by obedience, he carries out His command" (*STh* II–II, q.161, a.6).

The Lord of heaven and earth delights to reveal Himself not to those who seek to dominate truth, but to those who receive it with gratitude. The Gospel's wisdom is not achieved but accepted.

Christ's invitation follows naturally: "Come to me, all you who labor and are burdened, and I will give you rest." This is not a rest from labor, but a rest *within* labor—the peace that flows from communion with God. Aquinas comments that this rest "consists in the peace and sweetness of the Holy Spirit, who inwardly comforts the faithful and assures them of their salvation" (*Commentary on Matthew*, 11:29).

For Aquinas, such rest is the fulfillment of the soul's desire. "Man's ultimate end is rest in God" (*STh* I–II, q.1, a.8). Every human striving—our search for meaning, for security, for peace—finds its true goal not in achievement but in union with the divine will. This is why the yoke of Christ is "easy": not because it demands less, but because it is borne in love.

"Love makes light whatever is heavy," writes Aquinas. "If the will loves something, then labor and pain themselves become sweet" (*STh* I–II, q.26, a.3, ad 2). The yoke of Christ transforms burden into beatitude, toil into trust, because it is shared with the One who is Love itself.

Zechariah's prophecy speaks of a humble king, "meek and riding on an ass." This is the paradox of divine kingship: omnipotence clothed in meekness. Aquinas notes that "meekness moderates anger and preserves peace" (*STh* II–II, q.157, a.1). It is the virtue of those who possess their strength rather than are possessed by it. Christ's meekness, then, is not weakness but perfect self-possession—a manifestation of divine love in human form.

This kenosis, this self-emptying, is not only the pattern of Calvary but the rhythm of divine life itself. To enter the meek and humble heart of Christ is to enter into Trinitarian communion, where love gives, receives, and returns in perfect peace. The rest Jesus promises is, ultimately, the rest of participation in that eternal love.

To be Christian is to be a disciple of divine humility. "Learn from me, for I am meek and humble of heart." Aquinas teaches that "the example of Christ's humility and suffering is the greatest incitement to patience" (*STh* III, q.46, a.3, ad 3). The more we contemplate His humility, the more our hearts are freed from the tyranny of self.

This humility is not a psychological strategy but a theological grace. It draws us into the very mystery of the Incarnation: the Word who became flesh so that our flesh might share in His divine rest. The humility of Christ is both revelation and redemption—it shows us who God is and heals who we are.

Let us, then, come to Him—empty, humble, and open. Let us lay down the burdens of pride, self-reliance, and control. Let us take up His yoke, the yoke of love that lightens every load. For "the end of all human desire," Aquinas says, "is to rest in the vision of God, which alone gives perfect satisfaction" (*STh* I–II, q.3, a.8).

This is the rest our hearts long for—the rest of the meek and humble, the peace of those who find themselves only by surrendering to Christ.

Fifteenth Sunday in Ordinary Time

Today's Gospel offers us one of Christ's most beloved parables—the Parable of the Sower. Our Lord, the Eternal Word made flesh, speaks not in abstractions but in the language of creation: of seed, soil, sun, and rain. The One through whom all things were made now reveals how the Word takes root within the heart. Here, divine revelation meets the drama of human freedom.

Through Isaiah, God had already prepared us: "As the rain and the snow come down from heaven and do not return there until they have watered the earth... so shall my word be that goes forth from my mouth; it shall not return to me empty" (Is 55:10–11). The Word of God is effective. It possesses within itself the power to bring about what it proclaims.

Saint Thomas Aquinas reflects that "the Word of God is operative, not as a mere sound passing through the air, but as containing divine power to accomplish what it signifies" (*STh* I, q.34, a.3). Just as rain falls abundantly but produces fruit only where the soil is receptive, so the divine Word is always fertile—but its fruitfulness depends on the disposition of the hearer. The divine initiative is unfailing; what is needed is human cooperation.

The sower in the parable is Christ Himself, scattering the Word of the Kingdom with prodigal generosity. "The same seed is sown in all," Aquinas comments, "for the preaching of the Gospel is one, yet the fruit differs according to the disposition of those who hear" (*Catena Aurea*, on Matthew 13:3–8). The difference, then, is not in the seed but in the soil.

Christ describes four types of ground: the path, the rocky ground, the rocky ground, the thorny soil, and the good earth. These represent not categories of people fixed for eternity, but conditions of the human heart—conditions that can change by grace. For, as Aquinas teaches, "Grace does not destroy nature but perfects it" (*STh* I, q.1, a.8, ad 2). The hardened heart can be tilled by repentance; the shallow heart can be deepened by trial; the divided heart can be purified by detachment and sacramental life.

Each of us, then, is invited to examine the soil of our soul. The sower never ceases to cast His seed, but we must prepare the ground to receive it fruitfully.

This parable is a revelation of both grace and freedom. Grace always takes the first step: "It is God who works in us both to will and to accomplish" (*STh* I–II, q.111, a.2). Yet, as Aquinas insists, "The movement of free will is required for justification, because God does not justify us without us" (*STh* I–II, q.113, a.3). Divine grace is the cause; our cooperation is the condition.

This is why Our Lord ends the parable not with an explanation but with an exhortation: "He who has ears, let him hear." To hear in the biblical sense means to receive and obey, to let the Word take root in the will and bear fruit in action. The Word sown in us is not passive information—it is a living form that seeks to shape us into the image of Christ.

Saint Paul widens the horizon in the second reading: "Creation waits with eager longing for the revelation of the children of God." The fruitfulness of the Word in the human soul is not merely personal—it is cosmic. For Aquinas, "the sons of God cooperate with divine providence in governing creation" (*STh* I, q.22, a.3). When grace transforms the heart, it also contributes to the renewal of the world.

The tilling of the soul and the restoration of creation are bound together. The interior transformation wrought by the Word anticipates the final liberation of creation from decay. Every act of faith, hope, and charity participates in this divine renewal.

In the life of the Church, this parable has particular relevance today. The crisis is not that the Word is weak, but that hearts are distracted, divided, and unprepared. The Word is proclaimed; but will it be received, interiorized, and allowed to bear fruit?

Aquinas reminds us that "the preaching of the Gospel is the chief instrument by which faith is produced in man" (*STh* II–II, q.2, a.3). Yet for the Word to be fruitful, it must fall upon cultivated soil. Formation—especially priestly formation—is precisely the patient tilling of the human heart: prayer, asceticism, study, and the sacraments work together to deepen the soil so that the seed of divine truth may grow roots that endure.

In every Mass, the Divine Sower sows anew. He not only casts the seed of His Word into our ears but gives us the seed of His own Body and Blood in the Eucharist. "The effect of this sacrament," writes Aquinas, "is the transformation of man into Christ" (*STh* III, q.79, a.1). The Eucharist makes fruitful what the Word has planted; it completes in sacramental reality what was begun in hearing.

To receive the Eucharist is to become fertile ground for the Kingdom. But we must receive with faith, hope, and love—those theological virtues that make the soul good soil.

The Blessed Virgin Mary is the perfect image of the receptive heart—the soil in which the Word became flesh. In her *fiat*, the divine seed found the most fertile ground in all creation. Through her humility, the Word took root and bore the fruit of salvation for the world.

Let us then, like her, receive the Word with docility. Let us allow the Holy Spirit to till the soil of our hearts, to break open what is hard, to deepen what is shallow, to purify what is divided. Then, like Mary, our souls will magnify the Lord, and our lives will bear fruit—thirty, sixty, a hundredfold—for the glory of God and the salvation of the world.

Sixteenth Sunday in Ordinary Time

Today's Gospel gives us one of the most sobering and yet hope-filled of all the Lord's parables—the Parable of the Weeds among the Wheat. In it, Christ unveils the mystery of the Church's life in history: the Kingdom of Heaven is like a field sown with good seed by the Son of Man, yet secretly infiltrated by an enemy who scatters weeds among the wheat.

This is not a parable of despair, but of divine patience. It teaches us how God governs His Church and the world—not by eradicating all evil now, but by sustaining the good amid evil until the final harvest. "Let them grow together until harvest," says the Lord (Mt 13:30).

This patience of God is not weakness, nor indifference to evil. It is mercy ordered by wisdom. As the Book of Wisdom reminds us, "Though You are master of might, You judge with clemency, and with much lenience You govern us" (Wis 12:18). Saint Thomas Aquinas explains this truth with profound clarity: "Mercy without justice is the mother of dissolution; justice without mercy is cruelty" (*STh* I, q.21, a.4). In God, mercy and justice are one. His justice is always merciful, and His mercy always just.

The field, Christ tells us, is the world—but it is also an image of the Church. Within the visible body of believers grow both wheat and weeds, saints and sinners. This coexistence is permitted by divine providence for a time, so that the freedom of human hearts may be tested and purified.

Aquinas comments that the Lord "permits the wicked to live among the good so that the good may be exercised in patience and charity" (*Catena Aurea*, on Matthew 13:29). The presence of evil, then, is not evidence of God's absence, but a summons to virtue. The wheat must grow stronger in the midst of the weeds; the faithful must become more deeply rooted in grace as they live among those who resist it.

The temptation, both then and now, is to try to purify the field ourselves—to uproot what seems evil, to separate the Church into the pure and the impure. But the Master warns: "In gathering the weeds you might uproot the wheat along with them." Aquinas sees in this command the divine wisdom that protects both justice and hope: "Because men cannot see the hearts of others, it often happens that one thought to be a sinner is, in truth, predestined to grace" (*STh* I, q.23, a.7, ad 1).

We do not judge the harvest before its time. Only God sees perfectly; only God can separate perfectly.

Behind this parable lies the serene power of divine providence. The enemy acts, but not outside God's permission; his malice becomes, in the end, a means of God's mercy. Aquinas writes that "God permits evil to exist in order to bring good out of it" (*STh* I, q.2, a.3, ad 1). The weeds do not frustrate the sower's work—they become the dark background against which the light of grace shines more clearly.

Providence, then, does not mean that everything is good, but that everything can be used for the good by the One who orders all things wisely. This is the secret confidence of the saints: that no evil—whether moral corruption, scandal, or persecution—can destroy the divine plan.

If God's response to evil is patient mercy, then the Church's response must be the same. Saint Paul reminds us in today's second reading that "the Spirit comes to the aid of our weakness; for we do not know how to pray as we ought, but the Spirit Himself intercedes with inexpressible groanings" (Rom 8:26).

Aquinas comments that "the Holy Spirit moves us to pray, giving us an interior desire for the good which surpasses our understanding" (*STh* II–II, q.83, a.1, ad 2). The Spirit's groaning within the Church is the sound of God's mercy at work, interceding through our weakness. In the midst of confusion or scandal, the Church's most powerful act is not argument but adoration—her most perfect response to evil is intercession.

Every Mass, then, is the Church's deepest answer to the parable. Here, in the Eucharist, the Just One offers Himself for the unjust; the pure Wheat offers Himself for the field in which He grows. "The effect of this sacrament," writes Aquinas, "is the unity of the Mystical Body" (*STh* III, q.79, a.1). In the Eucharist, the Lord keeps the Church together, even when human frailty threatens to tear it apart.

Christ's parable also calls each of us to self-examination. The line dividing wheat and weed does not run between "us" and "them," but through every human heart. Within each of us lies the capacity for both fidelity and betrayal, grace and sin. Aquinas teaches that "the beginning of good in us is the movement of grace; its imperfection is from us, its perfection from God" (*STh* I–II, q.109, a.9).

Thus, the spiritual life is not about judging others but cooperating with grace within ourselves. To become wheat is to allow the divine life to mature in us—to be conformed ever more to Christ, who is the grain of wheat that fell into the earth and died, bearing fruit for our salvation (Jn 12:24).

At the end of the parable, Christ promises that at the harvest "the righteous will shine like the sun in the kingdom of their Father." Aquinas interprets this as a foretaste of the beatific vision: "In that glory the saints will participate in the brightness of God Himself, by seeing Him as He is" (*STh* I–II, q.3, a.8).

This is the hope that sustains the Church amid trial. The field may look mixed, the harvest delayed, the enemy active—but the final word belongs to the Lord of the harvest. His patience is not postponement; it is purpose. He is gathering, purifying, and perfecting His people through time, until His justice and mercy meet in the light of eternity.

We live in an age of confusion, scandal, and suffering in the Church. But despair and division are not the answer. The Lord is still sowing good seed. Our task is not to uproot others but to bear fruit ourselves—to deepen our fidelity, purify our love, and entrust the harvest to God.

"Patience," Aquinas says, "safeguards the good of reason against sorrow" (*STh* II–II, q.136, a.2). To live with patience is to live with faith—to believe that God's providence is not thwarted by evil, but at work even through it.

So let us strive to be rich soil and fruitful wheat. Let us pray for those who struggle, and intercede for those who err. Let us remain faithful to the Church even when she suffers from within. For the Lord sees all, governs all, and will one day bring all to light. He is patient because He is merciful. And He is coming.

Seventeenth Sunday in Ordinary Time

Today's Gospel presents us with three short but decisive parables about the Kingdom of Heaven: a man finds a treasure buried in a field; a merchant discovers a pearl of great price; a fisherman casts his net and separates what is valuable from what is not. Each parable confronts us with the same reality: the Kingdom of God is of such surpassing worth that it demands—and deserves—everything.

This is not a Gospel of comfort or compromise. It is the Gospel of the absolute. The Kingdom is worth all we have, not because God exacts a price, but because the gift itself is infinite. To gain it is to find the one thing that endures when all else passes away.

In our first reading, Solomon is given a divine invitation: "Ask for whatever you want." He could have asked for wealth, victory, or long life—but instead he prays for *a listening heart*, for wisdom to discern what is right (1 Kgs 3:9).

Saint Thomas Aquinas defines wisdom (*sapientia*) not as the possession of much knowledge, but as "the habit by which man judges rightly concerning divine things and orders all things toward their due end" (*STh* II–II, q.45, a.1). Wisdom is the light of right judgment illuminated by charity. Solomon's choice is therefore not pragmatic but theological: he chooses to see as God sees. He chooses to order his life toward the divine end. He chooses the pearl of great price.

This wisdom is both contemplative and practical. It reveals what truly matters and empowers us to act accordingly. As Aquinas writes, "It belongs to wisdom to direct human acts according to the order of divine reason" (*STh* II–II, q.45, a.6). To live wisely is to live rightly ordered—to let every choice flow from love of God as our final end.

The farmer and the merchant in the Gospel both see something extraordinary—and they act. Their decisions are not calculated but spontaneous, not reluctant but joyful: *"From joy over it he goes and sells all that he has and buys that field."*

Aquinas explains that the perfection of charity does not diminish joy but fulfills it, for "charity is the friendship of man for God" (*STh* II–II, q.23, a.1). To sell all is not an act of loss, but of love. The joy arises because the soul recognizes that what it gains—union with God—is infinitely more valuable than anything it surrenders.

This Gospel invites us to examine not what we possess, but what possesses us. The Kingdom cannot be one among many priorities; it must be the horizon against which all else is measured. To cling to lesser goods is to remain blind to the supreme good. "The act of charity," Aquinas says, "consists in loving God above all things and referring all other things to the love of Him" (*STh* II–II, q.27, a.4).

Why is the treasure hidden? Not because God wishes to conceal it from us, but because He desires to awaken our longing. "The Word of God," Aquinas observes, "is hidden from the wise and revealed to the humble" (*Catena Aurea*, on Matthew 11:25). The divine mystery is not grasped by analysis but received by love.

God does not force the Kingdom upon us; He draws us toward it through desire purified by sacrifice. The hiddenness of the treasure is pedagogical—it trains the heart to seek what is eternal. Aquinas explains that "the desire of the soul is not satisfied by created things, but only by the Creator" (*STh* I–II, q.2, a.8). Every lesser love is a shadow of the ultimate Love. The pearl of great price is God Himself, the uncreated Beauty who fulfills every human longing.

Thus, the joy of the man who sells all he has is not incidental—it is the natural overflow of a heart that has found its end. What he once saw as loss, he now knows as liberation.

These parables also speak directly to the work of formation—especially priestly and ecclesial formation. The spiritual life is not about accumulation, but about purification. The goal is not to possess many things but to be possessed by the one thing necessary (cf. Lk 10:42).

Aquinas reminds us that "charity is the form of all the virtues, because it directs the acts of all the virtues to their ultimate end, which is God" (*STh* I–II, q.65, a.2). True formation, then, is the ordering of the whole person toward the final end. Knowledge, ascetic discipline, pastoral skill—all are valuable only insofar as they are united by charity to the pursuit of God Himself.

The merchant in the Gospel does not seek pearls in general; he seeks *the pearl*. So too the disciple must not be distracted by secondary goods, no matter how noble, but must remain focused on the ultimate Good. For to serve the Kingdom requires a single heart, purified by love and sustained by hope.

The final parable reminds us that the Kingdom also has a future dimension. The net of the Gospel gathers "fish of every kind," and at the end of the age, "the angels will separate the wicked from the righteous."

Aquinas interprets this as an image of divine discernment: "The separation will be made not by external appearance but by the interior disposition of charity" (*Catena Aurea*, on Matthew 13:49). The final judgment, then, is not arbitrary. It is the full revelation of what each soul has freely chosen to love.

This gives meaning to the patient endurance of the Church's mission. The Kingdom is both already and not yet—already present in grace, but not yet consummated in glory. Until then, we live by faith, allowing the divine wisdom of God to reorder our loves and purify our desires.

The Gospel does not promise comfort, but it promises joy. The joy of the Kingdom is not the absence of sacrifice, but its transfiguration. "Joy," Aquinas says, "is caused by love; for when we love a person, it is a joy to be united to him" (*STh* I–II, q.31, a.3). The saints are joyful because they have found what every heart longs for—the treasure that does not fade, the pearl beyond price, the love that endures.

So today, let us renew our choice for the Kingdom. Let us not merely admire the treasure from afar but sell all we have—our pride, our attachments, our comforts—and follow Christ through the narrow gate. For what God offers is not one good among many; it is the Good itself.

To give everything for Him is not loss, but wisdom. For as Aquinas concludes, "In the vision of God consists man's perfect happiness, because He alone is the fulfillment of every desire" (*STh* I–II, q.3, a.8).

Eighteenth Sunday in Ordinary Time

Today we are drawn into two profound theophanies—two moments where God reveals Himself: one to Elijah on Mount Horeb, and the other to Peter and the disciples in the storm-tossed boat on the Sea of Galilee. In both cases, God reveals Himself not through overwhelming displays of cosmic power, but through His sovereign nearness—in the still small voice, and in the hand that reaches into the chaos and says, "Take courage; it is I; do not be afraid."

The first reading presents the prophet Elijah not as a triumphant champion, but as a man exhausted and disillusioned. He flees to Horeb, the mountain of God—the very place where Moses encountered the Lord in fire and cloud. Yet Elijah's theophany is not like Moses': "The Lord was not in the wind... not in the earthquake... not in the fire... but in a still small voice" (1 Kgs 19:11–12). The Hebrew phrase *qôl demamah daqqah* can also be rendered "a voice of thin silence." God reveals Himself in vulnerability, not violence; in intimacy, not intimidation.

Saint Thomas Aquinas teaches that God's mode of communication must be suited to the recipient: "Divine revelation accommodates itself to human weakness" (*STh* I, q.12, a.4). Elijah is no longer the prophet of fire on Mount Carmel; he is the weary servant who needs not to do, but to listen. And God comes to him in silence, to draw him back into communion.

In the Gospel, Jesus again reveals Himself in unexpected ways. After dismissing the crowds, He sends His disciples into the sea and ascends the mountain to pray—evoking Moses on Sinai and prefiguring His high priestly prayer. As the storm rises and the boat is battered by waves, Christ comes walking on the water, an epiphany rich in biblical symbolism. In Job 9:8, it is God who "treads upon the waves of the sea." This is no mere display of power—it is the revelation that Jesus is Lord over chaos, Lord over creation, Lord over fear.

The boat has long been seen as an image of the Church, tossed by the winds of persecution, false teaching, and interior doubt. Yet Christ comes to her. He does not abandon His Bride. The storm remains, but so does the presence of the One who says, "It is I"—literally in the Greek, *egō eimi*—echoing the divine name from the burning bush (Ex 3:14).

Peter, ever impetuous, steps out onto the sea. This gesture is both faith-filled and precarious. He begins well, but seeing the wind, he falters. Here we see the drama of the Christian life: to walk toward Christ in a world of storms. As Aquinas says, faith is not mere belief, but a movement of the intellect and will toward God under the impulse of grace (*STh* II–II, q.6, a.1). Peter's faith is genuine yet imperfect—and yet Christ does not abandon him. He reaches out immediately and saves him.

The Lord permits Peter to experience his weakness, not as punishment, but as purification. Only through sinking does Peter truly learn to cry out: "Lord, save me!" In this, the Church is taught how to walk—not with self-reliance, but with trust; not with worldly stability, but with supernatural courage. Christ does not always still the storm—but He is always present in it.

Paul's anguish in the second reading reminds us that not all will accept this presence. His lament over Israel's rejection of the Messiah echoes the pain of every evangelizer. He lists the privileges of Israel—covenants, promises, worship—but grieves that they have not yet recognized the fulfillment of all these things in Christ. And yet he does not despair.

Let us not fear the wind or the silence. The Lord comes in both. Let us be the Church that listens like Elijah and walks like Peter—imperfectly, yes, but with our eyes on Christ. And when we falter, let us cry out: "Lord, save me." For He is near, He is Lord, and He is love.

Nineteenth Sunday in Ordinary Time

Today's Gospel confronts us with one of the most arresting and unsettling scenes in the life of our Lord: a Gentile woman, a Canaanite, crying out in desperation—*"Have pity on me, Lord, Son of David!"*—and Jesus, initially, saying not a word. Then, when He does speak, He seems to rebuff her: *"It is not right to take the food of the children and throw it to the dogs."* How are we to understand this apparent hardness from the One who is Love incarnate?

The key to this text is found in understanding divine pedagogy. Saint Thomas Aquinas, commenting on this passage, teaches that Christ's apparent delay and refusal are not rejections, but a means of eliciting greater faith from the woman—and instruction for His disciples (*Catena Aurea*, Matthew 15). Jesus is not ignoring her; He is leading her into the fullness of her faith.

Notice what happens. She addresses Him first with a messianic title—*"Son of David."* But Jesus remains silent. Then, when she kneels and simply cries, *"Lord, help me,"*—a prayer of pure humility—He engages her. She responds, *"Even the dogs eat the scraps that fall from their masters' table."* Here, she demonstrates what Saint Augustine calls *"the humility that opens the gates of mercy."* Her faith is no longer based on borrowed titles or ethnic privilege. It is based on the recognition of Jesus' divine lordship and the overflowing abundance of His mercy.

This woman is, in fact, an icon of the Church. She is a Gentile, yet she believes. She is excluded, yet she perseveres. She comes on behalf of another—her tormented daughter—and so becomes a figure of intercession. She clings to the mercy of Christ, not out of entitlement, but out of desperate love. And Jesus praises her: *"O woman, great is your faith!"*

In the context of salvation history, this episode prefigures the ingrafting of the Gentiles into the covenant. As Saint Paul says in today's second reading, *"I glory in my ministry in order to make my race jealous and thus save some of them"*(Rom 11:13–14). Paul understands the mission to the Gentiles as part of God's mysterious plan of universal salvation. The gifts and the call of God are irrevocable—not only for Israel, but now for all peoples.

Isaiah foresaw this: *"The foreigners who join themselves to the Lord... them I will bring to my holy mountain"* (Isa 56:6–7). This prophecy is fulfilled in Christ, and most especially in the Eucharist—the *house of prayer for all peoples.* In the Church, through the sacraments, the promise made to Abraham—that all nations would be blessed—is now realized.

Saint Thomas explains that faith is both a theological virtue infused by grace (*STh* II-II, q.6, a.1) and a human act moved by God and assenting to the truth He reveals (*STh* II-II, q.2, a.1). The Canaanite woman exercises this virtue with exemplary clarity. She recognizes who Jesus is, believes in His power, and entrusts herself entirely to His mercy. She is not discouraged by delay or denial, but presses on. In this, she teaches us how to pray and how to trust. In an age where we often demand instant affirmation, this Gospel reminds us that perseverance in prayer is itself an act of sanctification.

Let us therefore imitate this woman. Let us intercede persistently for others. Let us approach the Lord not as consumers, but as beggars of grace. Let us pray not only with our lips but with hearts kneeling before the Lord, willing to receive whatever He gives—even if it seems at first to be only crumbs. For with Christ, even the crumbs are infinite.

And in the Eucharist, He does not give us crumbs. He gives us His very Self.

Twentieth Sunday in Ordinary Time

These words of the Lord Jesus to Simon Peter, spoken at Caesarea Philippi, are among the most foundational in all of Scripture for the Catholic understanding of the Church. They are not merely an honorific for Peter, but the institution of something utterly new: the visible headship of the apostolic college, the Petrine office, and ultimately the papacy.

The location is not incidental. Caesarea Philippi was a place known for pagan worship, built near a shrine to the Greek god Pan. It is in this context of competing worldviews that Jesus asks the most important question in human history: *"Who do you say that I am?"* (Mt 16:15). And Peter, by divine illumination, replies: *"You are the Christ, the Son of the living God."* This confession is not from flesh and blood, but from the Father. Jesus replies not simply with praise, but with institution: *"You are Peter, and on this rock I will build my Church."*

Here, we see the convergence of identity and mission. The name "Peter"—*Petros*, the rock—is not a poetic flourish, but a covenantal reality. Just as Abram became Abraham, and Jacob became Israel, so Simon becomes Peter: his identity transformed in light of a divine mission. As Saint Leo the Great preached, *"The privilege of Peter remains, wherever judgment is rightly passed. And wherever there is perseverance in what he decreed, there is the solidity of the Rock."*(*Sermon 3 on the Anniversary of His Consecration*)

To understand this in a theological light, we look to Isaiah 22 in our first reading, where the Lord says of Eliakim: *"I will place the key of the House of David on his shoulder."* This passage is the background for Jesus' own words about giving Peter *"the keys of the kingdom of heaven."* In the Davidic kingdom, the steward who held the key governed with the authority of the king. Christ, the Son of David, entrusts Peter with real authority to govern His Church. The Catechism of the Catholic Church affirms: *"The Pope, Bishop of Rome and Peter's successor, is the perpetual and visible source and foundation of the unity both of the bishops and of the whole company of the faithful"* (CCC §882).

Saint Thomas Aquinas, in his *Commentary on Matthew* and the *Summa Theologiae*, explains that Peter's confession expresses the perfection of faith: "In this confession, there is contained both the humanity and divinity of Christ," and therefore, it is the solid foundation upon which the Church must be built (*STh* III, q.16, a.1, ad 2). Christ is the true Rock (*1 Cor 10:4*), but He chooses to build His Church on the instrumentality of Peter to safeguard unity, orthodoxy, and continuity.

This truth is not only ecclesiological but deeply pastoral. Peter was no stranger to failure. He would falter, deny, and weep bitterly. Yet Christ still chose him—not because of Peter's natural strength, but because of the supernatural grace of his confession and his vocation. The papacy, then, is not an office of perfection, but of grace-imbued service, a visible sign that Christ does not abandon His Church. The Pope is not above the Church, but within her, as servant of the servants of God.

For those of us in priestly or theological formation, Peter's example is both bracing and consoling. Bracing, because it reminds us that ecclesial office is always ordered to confession of Christ and self-emptying service. Consoling, because it shows that Christ uses fragile vessels—so long as they cling to Him with faith.

And for all the faithful, this Gospel teaches that the Church is not a human invention, but a divine institution. Amid crises and scandals, we must never forget that Christ, not man, is the builder. The gates of hell will not prevail—not because of our strategies, but because of His promise.

Let us therefore renew our love for the Church, founded on Peter but sustained by Christ. Let us pray for the Holy Father, Pope Leo XIV, that he may be a faithful steward of the keys. And let us echo Peter's confession, not only with our lips but with our lives: *"You are the Christ, the Son of the living God."*

Twenty-First Sunday in Ordinary Time

Last Sunday, we heard Peter make his great confession: *"You are the Christ, the Son of the living God"* (Mt 16:16). This Sunday, we hear him rebuke the very Christ he had just confessed. *"God forbid, Lord! No such thing shall ever happen to you!"* (Mt 16:22). What a difference seven verses make. From *"Blessed are you, Simon,"* to *"Get behind me, Satan!"*

This startling reversal reveals a truth at the heart of the Christian life: it is not enough to confess Christ in word—we must also accept the mystery of His Cross.

Peter's error is not doctrinal, but existential. He rightly identified Jesus as the Messiah, but misunderstood what kind of Messiah He is. He recoils from the notion that the Christ must suffer and be killed. He wants resurrection without crucifixion, glory without sacrifice. In this, he unwittingly becomes an obstacle. *"You are a stumbling block to me,"* says the Lord. The Greek word *skandalon* refers to something that causes another to trip. Ironically, Peter—the rock— is now the stumbling stone.

Saint Thomas Aquinas, commenting on this passage, notes that Peter's rebuke is a temptation similar to that offered by Satan in the desert: a kingdom without the Cross, glory without obedience. But Jesus, the New Adam, remains faithful to the mission entrusted to Him by the Father (*STh* III, q.46, a.4).

This Gospel, then, is not merely about Peter—it is about us. For Jesus goes on to say: *"If anyone wishes to come after me, he must deny himself, take up his cross, and follow me"* (Mt 16:24). This is not a metaphor for discomfort or disappointment. The cross is the form of

Christian life. It is the shape of love in a fallen world. And the disciple must conform himself to the crucified Lord, not only in outward suffering but in inward self-offering.

Here Saint Paul's words in the second reading are decisive: *"Offer your bodies as a living sacrifice, holy and pleasing to God—your spiritual worship"* (Rom 12:1). The word he uses—*logikēn latreian*—can be rendered "rational worship" or "logically fitting worship." For Aquinas, this is the heart of the moral life: the transformation of the person through grace to offer his entire self to God as a reasonable act of love (*STh* II-II, q.81, a.1).

This sacrificial worship is not confined to the altar—it is to become the rhythm of our daily lives. The Christian is not conformed to this age, but transformed by the renewal of the mind (*Rom 12:2*), shaped by divine truth rather than worldly convenience. In a culture of self-assertion and spiritual mediocrity, the Cross remains a scandal. But for those who believe, it is the wisdom and power of God.

The prophet Jeremiah, in our first reading, speaks with raw honesty: *"You duped me, O Lord, and I let myself be duped… I say I will not mention him, I will speak in his name no more. But then it becomes like fire burning in my heart"* (Jer 20:7, 9). This is the interior cost of prophetic fidelity. Every true vocation bears the mark of the Cross—not as punishment, but as participation in the love that redeems the world.

For those of us called to follow Christ in ordained ministry, consecrated life, or Christian discipleship in the world, today's Gospel is a summons to ongoing conversion. We must move from confessing Christ merely with our lips to embracing Him with our lives—even, and especially, when He leads us to Calvary.

Let us not be scandalized by the Cross. Let us not rebuke what God has willed. Let us deny ourselves, take up our cross daily, and follow Him—not out of fear, but out of love. For only in losing our life for His sake will we find it.

Twenty-Second Sunday in Ordinary Time

Today's readings speak with clarity and urgency about the responsibility of fraternal correction and the bonds of love that hold the Christian community together. They teach us that Christian charity is not sentimentality, but truth in love; not silence in the face of sin, but a willingness to speak with courage, humility, and mercy.

The prophet Ezekiel receives a solemn charge from the Lord: *"You, son of man, I have appointed watchman for the house of Israel"* (Ez 33:7). The watchman must speak. Silence in the face of moral danger is not discretion—it is complicity. Aquinas, commenting on this prophetic task, notes that "to reprove the sinner is a spiritual work of mercy and an act of fraternal charity" (*STh* II-II, q.33, a.1). The obligation to admonish is not optional. It is an essential dimension of love rightly ordered.

Saint Paul deepens this in today's second reading: *"Owe nothing to anyone, except to love one another"* (Rom 13:8). This love is not abstract; it is concrete, rooted in the commandments. Love fulfills the law not by negating moral truth, but by perfecting it. Aquinas affirms that "the whole Law is contained in the love of God and neighbor, because charity is the form of the virtues" (*STh* II-II, q.23, a.8). Hence, true love never tolerates sin as if it were a minor flaw, but seeks the salvation of the other.

In the Gospel, our Lord gives a precise and graduated process for fraternal correction. It is profoundly ecclesial. First, go privately. Then, bring two or three witnesses. Finally, bring it to the Church. The goal is always restoration, never humiliation. It is a pedagogy of mercy ordered toward reconciliation. And the final phrase—*"treat him as you would a Gentile or a tax collector"* (Mt 18:17)—must be read not as dismissal, but as Christ Himself treated such persons: with missionary zeal and redemptive hope.

Christ's words conclude with the astonishing promise: *"Whatever you bind on earth shall be bound in heaven"* (Mt 18:18). This is not only addressed to Peter, as in Matthew 16, but to the Church. It expresses the ecclesial authority to forgive, to discipline, and to heal. The Church is not a spiritual club but a sacramental communion with real bonds of accountability. The community of the baptized is responsible for one another.

This Gospel is particularly relevant today in an age that often confuses tolerance with love and reduces mercy to mere affirmation. In a Church marked by synodality and shared responsibility, this task belongs not only to pastors but to all the faithful.

Yet we must be clear: correction must be guided by love and humility. Saint Augustine warns that one must correct "not as an adversary, but as a physician; not as a foe, but as a father." We speak not to condemn, but to invite. We do not react with anger but respond with the charity that seeks the other's good. If we rebuke in pride, we become the very scandal we are trying to heal.

And the heart of all this is prayer. *"If two of you agree on earth about anything for which they are to pray, it shall be granted to them by my heavenly Father"* (Mt 18:19). Correction, reconciliation, and ecclesial communion are rooted in shared intercession. Where two or three are gathered in His name, there is Christ—especially when the gathering is marked by the pursuit of truth and peace.

For those in formation—whether seminarians, religious, or lay ministers—this Gospel is especially formative. Pastoral charity requires the courage to correct, the prudence to discern when and how, and the humility to recognize one's own sinfulness. In the model of Christ, the Good Shepherd, we correct not from above, but from beside; not as masters, but as servants of grace.

Let us therefore not grow indifferent to one another's salvation. Let us not fear to speak the truth in love, nor delay in seeking reconciliation. For where charity and truth meet, there is Christ. And in the heart of the Church, bound together in the grace of fraternal communion, we shall find not only correction—but healing.

Twenty-Third Sunday in Ordinary Time

"Lord, if my brother sins against me, how often must I forgive him? As many as seven times?" (Mt 18:21).

Peter's question is sincere. It reflects a generous impulse—a willingness to go beyond the common rabbinic teaching that three acts of forgiveness would suffice. But Jesus responds with a command that transcends all calculation: "I do not say to you seven times, but seventy-seven times." That is to say, always.

To forgive is to imitate God. And to withhold forgiveness is to cut oneself off from divine life.

The parable that follows—the Parable of the Unforgiving Servant—is one of the most striking illustrations of divine mercy and human hardness of heart. The servant is forgiven a debt so massive it is almost unimaginable—ten thousand talents, the equivalent of billions of dollars in today's currency. But he refuses to forgive a fellow servant who owes him only a fraction of that—a hundred denarii. The imbalance is deliberate. Jesus wants us to see the scandal of a forgiven sinner refusing to forgive.

The first reading from Sirach anticipates this truth centuries earlier: "Could anyone nourish anger against another and expect healing from the Lord?" (Sir 28:3). This is not a rhetorical question; it is a spiritual law. Forgiveness is not optional. It is the condition for receiving divine mercy. We pray it every day: "Forgive us our trespasses, as we forgive those who trespass against us."

Saint Thomas Aquinas notes that this petition of the Lord's Prayer expresses not only a desire but a kind of judgment upon ourselves—we are asking God to treat us according to the same measure with which we treat others (*STh* II–II, q.83, a.9). Forgiveness, then, is not simply a moral ideal; it is a divine necessity. The heart that refuses to forgive cannot truly receive mercy because it remains closed.

But we must be honest—true forgiveness is not easy. It is one of the hardest commands of the Gospel. When the wounds are deep, when betrayal has cut to the heart, forgiveness can seem impossible. Yet the Lord does not ask us to pretend that sin does not hurt. He invites us instead to place our pain within the larger horizon of the Cross. From the Cross, Christ does not wait for apologies. He prays, "Father, forgive them." This is the measure of Christian love—not justice as the world defines it, but mercy that heals and transforms.

Saint Paul reminds us in the second reading of the foundation for all Christian forgiveness: "Whether we live or die, we are the Lord's" (Rom 14:8). The one who has been redeemed cannot live for himself. If Christ died for our enemies, then we must die to our pride, our resentment, and our desire for revenge. Only then can we live in true freedom.

Aquinas reminds us that the perfection of charity is found in willing the good of the other as God wills it (*STh* II–II, q.23, a.1). To forgive, then, is an act of love ordered by grace—it is to desire the restoration and healing of the one who has wronged us. It is a participation in the charity of Christ Himself, who loves even those who wound Him.

This Gospel also speaks directly to those who serve the Church— priests, religious, and lay leaders. Ministry inevitably involves woundedness—sometimes received, sometimes caused. Yet those who bear the Gospel must always be ministers of reconciliation. The credibility of the Church does not lie in perfection, but in the willingness to forgive and to be forgiven. The shepherd must forgive seventy-seven times—not merely from duty, but out of love for the Good Shepherd.

Forgiveness is not forgetting. It is not pretending evil never happened. It is a grace-filled decision not to let evil define the future. It is the liberation of the heart from the prison of resentment. And it is a participation in the very life of the Trinity, whose inner life is one of perfect mercy and communion.

So today, the Lord places before us a question even deeper than Peter's: Am I willing to forgive as I have been forgiven? If not, we risk becoming like the unforgiving servant—imprisoned not by God's wrath, but by our own unwillingness to be free.

Let us, then, come to this altar in humility. Let us lay down our debts and our grievances. And let us receive, once more, the infinite mercy of the Crucified Christ—so that we may become agents of reconciliation in a world starving for peace.

Twenty-Fourth Sunday in Ordinary Time

Today's Gospel presents us with one of the most surprising and, at first, disorienting parables in all of Scripture—the Parable of the Laborers in the Vineyard. At first glance, it seems to offend our innate sense of justice. How can those who worked only one hour receive the same wage as those who bore "the day's burden and the heat"? And yet, this is precisely the point. The Kingdom of Heaven does not operate according to the logic of human merit, but according to the mystery of divine grace.

In the parable, the landowner—who represents God—goes out again and again to seek laborers, even up to the eleventh hour. His generosity is not conditioned by what the laborers can earn, but by His desire that they be included in the work and rewarded with what He alone can give. The vineyard is not a place of competition, but of communion.

This is why the parable is not really about economics—it is about grace. As the first reading from Isaiah reminds us, "My thoughts are not your thoughts, nor are your ways my ways" (Isa 55:8). Divine justice is not retributive, but restorative. It seeks not to give each according to strict desert, but to draw all into the joy of participation in the Kingdom. God is not a contract negotiator—He is a Father.

Saint Thomas Aquinas, reflecting on the order of grace, teaches that while nature operates according to fixed laws, grace is always superabundant and freely given (*STh* I–II, q.109, a.2). It cannot be measured in hours worked or positions held. The early laborers are not wronged by receiving the promised denarius—they are invited to see that God's generosity to others does not diminish His faithfulness to them.

This parable also offers a powerful meditation on vocation. Whether one is called in the morning of life or in the twilight hour, the reward is the same: union with Christ. Those called to the priesthood, religious life, or apostolic service must never see their vocation as a wage to be tallied, but as a gift to be lived. And those who discover the call to holiness later in life are not second-class disciples—they are full inheritors of the Kingdom.

This is especially consoling for those who feel they have come late to faith. The eleventh-hour worker is not shamed—he is welcomed. The Church is not a meritocracy but a communion of grace. God's generosity knows no timetable; His mercy is not diminished by its abundance.

Saint Paul, in our second reading, expresses this same truth: "For to me, life is Christ, and death is gain" (Phil 1:21). His concern is not the length of his service, but the depth of his love. Whether in labor or in death, what matters is that Christ be glorified in the body.

Yet, this Gospel also warns us. The temptation of the early laborers is real. They agreed to the work and the wage, but grumbled when the last received as much. Their complaint reveals a transactional heart: "We deserve more." But divine love cannot be bargained. If we see our service to the Church as a means of earning status, reward, or recognition, we risk becoming like those who labored much but loved little.

Aquinas reminds us that charity is the form of all the virtues—it gives meaning and value to every act (*STh* II–II, q.23, a.8). Without charity, even the hardest labor becomes empty. But when love animates our work, even the smallest act becomes eternal.

For those in formation—whether seminarians, religious, or lay leaders—this parable is especially vital. Our work in the vineyard is not measured by hours or accolades, but by fidelity to the call. The humility to rejoice in the generosity shown to others is a mark of spiritual maturity. The ability to serve without comparison, and to labor without envy, is the sign of a true disciple.

Let us then not look at what others have received, but at what we have been given. Let us thank the Lord that we have been called at all—whether early or late—to labor in the vineyard of grace. And let us rejoice that the wage we receive is not a payment, but a Person: Jesus Christ, the generous Lord of the harvest.

Twenty-Fifth Sunday in Ordinary Time

Today's Gospel presents one of the most surprising and challenging parables in all of Scripture—the Parable of the Laborers in the Vineyard. At first hearing, it seems to offend our natural sense of fairness. How can those who worked only one hour receive the same wage as those who labored all day in the hot sun? Yet this is precisely the point. The Kingdom of Heaven does not operate according to human logic or merit—it operates according to the mystery of divine grace.

In the parable, the landowner—who represents God—goes out again and again, even to the very end of the day, to invite more workers into his vineyard. His generosity is not conditioned by how much the laborers can earn, but by His desire that they share in His work and receive what only He can give. The vineyard is not a place of competition; it is a place of communion.

This parable is not about economics—it is about grace. As we heard in the first reading from Isaiah: "My thoughts are not your thoughts, nor are your ways my ways" (Isa 55:8). God's justice is not about repayment, but restoration. He does not divide His blessings by merit; He pours them out to bring all people into His joy. God is not a contract negotiator—He is a Father whose love always exceeds expectation.

Saint Thomas Aquinas reminds us that while nature follows fixed laws, grace is always superabundant and freely given (*STh* I–II, q.109, a.2). Grace cannot be measured in hours worked or in titles held. The early laborers are not cheated when they receive what was promised—they are invited to see that God's generosity toward others does not lessen His goodness to them.

This parable is also a meditation on vocation. Whether one is called early in life or at the final hour, the reward is the same: union with Christ. Those called to priesthood, religious life, marriage, or apostolic service must not see their vocation as a wage to be counted, but as a gift to be lived. And those who find their faith later in life are not lesser disciples—they are full heirs to the Kingdom of God.

This truth brings deep consolation to anyone who feels they have come late to the Lord. The worker hired at the eleventh hour is not shamed—he is welcomed. The Church is not a meritocracy; it is a communion of grace. God's generosity knows no timetable; His mercy is not diminished by its abundance.

In the second reading, Saint Paul expresses the same spirit when he writes, "For to me, life is Christ, and death is gain" (Phil 1:21). His concern is not the length of his service, but the fruitfulness of his love. What matters is that Christ be glorified—in our work, in our suffering, in our life and death.

But this Gospel also warns us. The temptation of the early laborers is real. They agreed to the work and the wage, but they grumbled when the last received the same. Their complaint reveals a heart that keeps score: "We deserve more." Yet God's love cannot be bargained. If we serve in the Church for recognition, reward, or prestige, we risk becoming like those who labored much but loved little.

Aquinas teaches that charity gives meaning and value to all our works—it is the form of every virtue (*STh* II–II, q.23, a.8). Without charity, even great effort becomes empty. But when love animates our labor, even small acts become eternal.

For those in formation—seminarians, religious, or lay leaders—this parable is especially important. Our work in the vineyard is not measured by hours, productivity, or praise, but by fidelity to the call. The humility to rejoice in the generosity shown to others is a mark of spiritual maturity. The ability to serve without envy and to labor without calculation is the sign of a true disciple.

Let us not fix our eyes on what others have received, but on what we have been given. Let us thank the Lord that we have been called at all—whether early or late—to labor in the vineyard of grace. And may our joy always be found, not in the wage we earn, but in the mercy we receive.

Twenty-Sixth Sunday in Ordinary Time

Today's Gospel presents us with a scene that pierces to the heart of Christian discipleship: the Parable of the Two Sons. One says, "I will not," but later obeys. The other says, "I will, sir," but does not go. The parable is not difficult to understand; what is difficult is the honesty it demands of us.

This parable, like so many of Christ's, turns our expectations inside out. Those who appear righteous—those who say the right words—are revealed to be disobedient. Those who appear defiant—tax collectors and prostitutes—are shown to have a capacity for conversion that far exceeds what the religious elite expected.

Saint Thomas Aquinas, commenting on Christ's teachings in the *Catena Aurea*, reminds us that "the righteousness of the Pharisees was in word only, while the repentance of sinners was in deed." True obedience is not found in empty piety but in concrete turning to the will of the Father.

But the parable is not simply moralistic. It draws us into the inner drama of grace and human freedom. The human response to God always takes place within a "theodramatic" structure: we are not authors of our own lives but characters in the great drama of God's redemptive love. The two sons represent two possible roles in this drama: the one who resists and then yields, and the one who assents with his lips but withdraws his heart.

The tragedy of the second son is precisely that he *says* yes, but does not *enter* into the action of grace. The "yes" of Christian life is not a verbal formula—it is a lived, cruciform reality.

The kenosis of Christ as the ultimate reversal of appearances. He who is equal to God does not cling to status, but empties Himself, becoming obedient *unto death—even death on a Cross* (Phil 2:6–11). All true obedience begins with listening (*obedire*—to hear) and ends in self-offering. This is what the first son ultimately does—he hears, he repents, he obeys.

Modern man often believes that saying the right thing—signaling virtue—is the same as being good. But for Christ, authenticity is not in words alone but in the hidden life of conversion. We can't have a "comfortable Christianity" that avoids the radical call of the Gospel by hiding behind external religiosity.

This parable, then, is not about two *kinds* of people, as though we could identify the "first sons" and the "second sons" around us. It is about each one of us. Within every human heart there is both resistance and assent. There is the capacity to say no and later be pierced by grace. There is also the temptation to perform obedience without interior conversion.

In today's first reading, the prophet Ezekiel insists: "*When the wicked turns away from the wickedness he has committed and does what is right and just, he shall preserve his life*" (Ez 18:27). The turning—*teshuvah* in Hebrew—is what God desires. This is not moralism; it is mercy. God does not delight in the fall of the sinner but rejoices in his return.

For us today, particularly those engaged in priestly or theological formation, this parable is a profound call to integrity. The true priest, the true disciple, is not the one who says "yes" most eloquently, but the one who enters most deeply into the obedience of the Son. This obedience is not without struggle. It often begins with resistance—like the first son—but it must end in surrender.

And let us not forget that Christ Himself is the Son who says Yes—not in pretense, but in total gift. *"Behold, I come to do your will, O God"* (Heb 10:9). In the Eucharist, we are united to that perfect obedience, that perfect self-offering. The Mass is not our performance of righteousness—it is our entrance into the Yes of the Son to the Father.

Let us then ask ourselves today: Are there areas of my life where I say "yes" to God in word but not in deed? Am I resisting the deeper conversion He asks of me? And, most importantly, am I willing to be changed—not by my own strength, but by the power of the obedience of Christ?

Let us imitate the first son. Let our "no" become a "yes" through repentance. Let our "yes" become a life of faithful obedience. And let our lives become, as Saint Paul says, a kenotic offering, patterned after the Cross, so that Christ may be all in all.

Twenty-Seventh Sunday in Ordinary Time

Today's Gospel confronts us with one of the most sobering parables of the Lord: the Parable of the Wicked Tenants. It is a story of patient love spurned, of stewardship betrayed, and of judgment rendered—not in anger, but in justice. It is also, profoundly, a mirror held up to the vineyard of the Church in every generation.

The Lord begins with an echo of Isaiah's "Song of the Vineyard": *"Let me sing for my beloved... My beloved had a vineyard on a fertile hill"* (Is 5:1). This vineyard is Israel—chosen, cultivated, and loved. But it yielded not justice, but bloodshed. The Hebrew uses wordplay: *mishpat* (justice) and *mispach* (bloodshed); *zedakah* (righteousness) and *ze'akah* (cry of distress). The point is painfully clear: when the people of God forget their vocation, they become a contradiction.

Christ takes up this theme and intensifies it. The landowner—the Father—sends servants (the prophets), and finally, *"his son,"* saying, *"They will respect my son."* But they kill him. In this, Jesus does not simply foretell His Passion; He interprets it. He is not a victim of accident but the rejected cornerstone, whose death paradoxically becomes the foundation of salvation: *"The stone that the builders rejected has become the cornerstone"* (Mt 21:42, Ps 118:22).

God's self-revelation is not only spoken but enacted—dramatically. The vineyard is the stage upon which God entrusts His beauty and goodness to human freedom. The tragic irony is that the Son—the very image of the Father—is cast out and slain. Yet this rejection is the turning point of salvation history. The drama descends into death, so that from death life may rise.

This parable can be read through the lens of Trinitarian obedience. The Son comes not merely as emissary but as *Gift*. He is the one who allows Himself to be handed over, who enters the vineyard not to enforce the Father's will but to bear its rejection in His own flesh. The Son, she says, "is obedience incarnate, even when obedience means walking into death with open eyes." This is not passive submission—it is a voluntary participation in the Father's redeeming plan.

The vineyard is ultimately a symbol of the people of God—the *ecclesia*. The parable is not only addressed to the chief priests and Pharisees of first-century Jerusalem; it speaks to every age of the Church. "The Kingdom of God will be taken away from you and given to a people that will produce its fruit" (Mt 21:43). This is not replacement but responsibility. The Church is not the vineyard *instead of* Israel, but the vineyard *as fulfilled* in Christ. She is fruitful only to the extent that she remains united to the rejected and risen Cornerstone.

Saint Thomas Aquinas, in his *Catena Aurea*, observes that this parable speaks not just of judgment but of *translatio regni*—the transfer of responsibility. The Kingdom is not destroyed, but it is entrusted anew—to those who will bear fruit in season. For Aquinas, the fruit is charity, the form of all the virtues, rooted in grace. Without love, the vineyard becomes a desolate field.

This homily is especially relevant for those engaged in ecclesial and priestly formation. The vineyard is the Church. We are the tenants. The vineyard is not our possession; it is our stewardship. Too often, ministries become possessions, offices become status, and charisms become grounds for division. But the Son comes among us still—especially in the Eucharist—and asks, *"Will you receive me?"*

The Church bears fruit only when she receives the Son in love and shares Him in sacrifice.

There is an ecclesial Pelagianism" that attempts to build the Church with human effort, rather than receiving her as a gift. The vineyard cannot be engineered; it must be cultivated through prayer, humility, and fidelity to the Word and sacraments. And every one of us must ask: *Am I producing fruit, or merely occupying the vineyard?*

Let us remember: the Son was cast out of the vineyard—He died *outside the gate* (Heb 13:12)—so that the whole world might become the new vineyard of grace. From His death springs the Church. From the rejected stone arises the foundation of a new humanity.

Let us then receive Him anew. Let us not grasp at the vineyard, but serve in it. Let our lives bear fruit—justice, holiness, mercy, charity. For only in receiving the Son can we remain in the vineyard. And only in union with the Cross can we become the fruitful Church the Father desires.

The parable of the vineyard is not merely a moral exhortation— it is, in the language of Hans Urs von Balthasar, a *theodrama*, a stage on which the divine and human wills meet, clash, and—by grace— may be reconciled. It is essential that we, especially as ministers and theologians, read this parable not as detached observers, but as actors already inserted into the scene.

The drama of salvation is not static doctrine but *enacted truth.* Christ, the Son, is not merely a messenger or representative—He is the divine Actor who plays the central role by *taking upon Himself the failure of the vineyard.* The tenants kill Him thinking to possess the inheritance, but in a paradox only divine wisdom can engineer, it is through this very rejection that the inheritance is made universal: *"God has consigned all to disobedience, that He might have mercy upon all"* (Rom 11:32).

Here we must deepen our understanding of divine *judgment*. Judgment is not primarily juridical, but *Christological*. The judgment of the tenants is not separate from the Son's death—it is *revealed* in it. The Father does not send armies to destroy the tenants in some future divine reaction. Rather, He allows the Son to enter into their rejection, and it is within this abyss that judgment and mercy are enacted.

The Cross is therefore the judgment of the world: it exposes the truth of sin (that we reject the Son), but also the greater truth of divine love (that God permits this rejection in order to save us). The Son is not only obedient but *open*. He enters the vineyard not with force, but with the vulnerability of the obedient one who is love itself: "The Son allows Himself to be handed over again and again, without resistance, because this is the rhythm of Trinitarian love."

From the Cross rises the new vineyard: the Church. Yet this Church remains fragile, because it remains human. This parable speaks not only of the transition from Israel to the Church but of the constant need for purification *within the Church*.

The vineyard must continually be renewed—not by restructuring or ideological reinvention, but by *conformity to the Son*. Only when the Church receives the Son—especially in the Eucharist—does she remain the fruitful vineyard.

Here the Eucharist becomes the decisive moment of ecclesial discernment. In every Mass, the Son is "sent into the vineyard" again. We, the tenants, receive Him. Will we welcome Him? Will we recognize His voice in the poor, the suffering, the unborn, the disfigured face of truth? Or will we seek to control the vineyard under the guise of piety, productivity, or politics?

The Church is *born from the side of Christ* as Eve from Adam, and that her mission is to bear the fruit of His Passion. That fruit is not success, growth, or applause. It is holiness. It is souls. It is the glory of the Father.

The "new tenants" must always be aware that they are *not owners but receivers*. Their role is to cultivate the fruit of the Son's obedience in the lives of others. This is why the priest, the bishop, the theologian, and the catechist must never view ministry as ownership but as Eucharistic participation: *"Do this in memory of me"* is not just a liturgical command—it is a summons to die in the vineyard, like the Son, that others may live.

Dear brothers and sisters, we are living in a time when the Church must again be purified—not by strategy but by sanctity. The Lord is once more sending His Son—hidden under the species of bread and wine, speaking through the Church's magisterium, crying out in the wounded of the world. Will we receive Him?

The Father is looking for fruit. The fruit He desires is the fruit of the Cross: obedience, love, fidelity, martyrdom—both red and white. Let us take up our place in this divine drama. Let us not fear judgment, for judgment in Christ is always the *judgment of love*. And let us labor in the vineyard with Eucharistic fidelity, knowing that only in union with the Crucified and Risen Son will our lives bear fruit that will last.

Twenty-Eighth Sunday in Ordinary Time

Today, our Lord presents us with another parable of judgment—but a judgment clothed in joy. The Kingdom is not described as a courtroom or a battlefield, but as a wedding feast. This image, drawn from the prophets and culminating in Revelation, is the definitive symbol of God's covenantal love: a nuptial banquet, prepared by the Father, for the Son, to which we are all invited.

Yet the drama of this parable lies in the shocking response of the invited guests: *they refuse to come.* Some are indifferent; others are violent. And even among those who come, one arrives without a wedding garment, and is cast out. This parable, then, is not merely about inclusion—it is about response, transformation, and the seriousness of grace.

In the first reading, the prophet Isaiah foretells a feast of rich food and choice wine (Is 25:6)—symbolizing God's eschatological promise to swallow death forever and wipe every tear from every face. In Christ, this prophecy is fulfilled in the Eucharist, where heaven touches earth and the Bridegroom feeds His Bride with His own Body and Blood.

The kingdom is not so much a place as a relationship—a communion. The feast is not earned; it is offered. But the invitation must be accepted in freedom. The tragedy of this parable is that those originally invited—symbolizing the leaders of Israel—prefer their fields and their business. The real scandal is not sin, but indifference. They treat the invitation as meaningless.

Modern man risks this same refusal—not out of malice, but by crowding out eternity with the urgency of temporal things. The

Gospel becomes background noise. But God's Kingdom is not a footnote to our agendas. It is the only thing that endures.

Then comes the second movement of the parable—perhaps even more mysterious. One man comes in, but without a wedding garment. He is speechless. And he is thrown out. What is this garment?

Saint Gregory the Great interpreted it as charity; Saint Augustine, as faith working through love. But Saint Thomas Aquinas, synthesizing both, teaches that the wedding garment is sanctifying grace, received and nurtured through the sacraments (*STh* III, q.62, a.3). One may be invited, may enter even visibly into the Church, and yet not be interiorly conformed to Christ. To come into the feast without grace is to be unprepared for communion.

Participation is crucial. One's entrance into the Kingdom is not passive acceptance but personal readiness to be drawn into the self-offering of the Son. The wedding garment is not an external accessory—it is the fabric of one's own participation in Christ's obedience, suffering, and glory. To wear it means to become a "living eucharistic being"—offered to the Father in union with the Son.

The garment represents our openness to receive the form of Christ. It is woven, she says, in silence, prayer, and surrender. The man without a garment is not judged for his past sins, but for his present refusal to be transformed. He has entered the Church but has not let the Church enter him.

The final warning—*"Many are called, but few are chosen"*—is not a threat but a wake-up call. The Church is the banquet hall where all are gathered—bad and good alike. But it is not enough to be present. The Gospel calls for conversion.

This parable reminds the Church that she is always under judgment—not because she lacks structure, but because she is accountable to grace. The wedding feast is Eucharistic. It is eschatological. And it is now.

Are we wearing the garment of grace? Are we helping others prepare for the feast? Are we treating the invitation with the gravity it deserves? This parable should shake us—but not into fear. Into holiness.

The Father has prepared the feast. The Eucharist is the foretaste of heaven. The invitation has gone out. What remains is our response.

Let us not be among those who treat the Gospel lightly. Let us not arrive unprepared. Let us, through daily repentance, sacramental life, and deep prayer, weave the wedding garment with our lives. Let us enter the nuptial feast not only as guests, but as friends of the Bridegroom—conformed to His love, clothed in His glory.

And let us never forget: this feast was made possible because the Bridegroom Himself was cast out—so that we might be welcomed in.

Twenty-Ninth Sunday in Ordinary Time

This well-known saying of our Lord is often reduced to a simple division between Church and State, as though Christ were endorsing a neat separation between the spiritual and the political. But the Gospel never deals in neat separations. It always calls us deeper, into the mystery where divine providence governs history, and where human freedom must be ordered to the truth.

In today's Gospel, the Pharisees and Herodians—ordinarily enemies—unite to trap Jesus. The question about paying taxes to Caesar is designed to force Him into a false dilemma. If He says yes, He appears a collaborator with the Roman occupiers; if He says no, He risks arrest for insurrection. But Christ, with divine authority, refuses their categories. He asks for a coin, points to the image engraved upon it, and says: *"Render to Caesar what is Caesar's, and to God what is God's."*

What is Caesar's? The coin—marked by his image, used for worldly exchange. What is God's? The human soul—marked by God's image, destined for eternal communion. This is not a lesson in civic duty; it is a call to radical discipleship.

Christ is not legitimizing Caesar's domain. He is relativizing it: "The State is not absolute. It belongs to a temporal order and must itself be judged in the light of God's eternal Kingdom." Whenever political power claims divine authority—whether in ancient Rome or modern totalitarianism—it becomes idolatrous. The Christian must render what is owed in justice, but never surrender what belongs to God alone: worship, conscience, and the final allegiance of the heart.

The deeper meaning of this Gospel lies in the word *image*. The coin bears Caesar's image—but the human person bears God's image (*imago Dei*). Saint Thomas Aquinas, following Augustine, teaches that man is "the image of God according to his mind" (*STh* I, q.93, a.6), capable of knowing, loving, and freely responding to God. To render to God what is God's is to give one's entire self, not merely what is religiously convenient.

The political and the spiritual are not separate spheres, but intersecting orders. In the first reading from Isaiah, God calls Cyrus—a pagan king—*"His anointed"*, the one through whom Israel's liberation will come. God's providence extends even to the "secular instruments" of salvation. History is not simply a backdrop for the sacred—it is the very field where divine and human freedom meet. The Church must never disengage from history, but must interpret it, sanctify it, and participate in it, not by dominance, but by fidelity.

God does not create "neutral zones." Every coin, every human act, every civic decision is either a path toward God or away from Him. There is no "middle ground" in the drama of salvation. To live as God's image-bearers is to be accountable—not just for interior belief, but for exterior witness, even under pressure from worldly powers.

The Church, then, is not an alternative empire, nor a private cult. She is the sacrament of Christ's Kingdom in the world—visible, real, and active, yet never reduced to earthly categories. When the Church becomes too politically aligned or too spiritually privatized, she loses her credibility. Her task is not to take Caesar's throne, but to form consciences, to proclaim truth, and to sanctify the world from within.

This task belongs especially to the laity, who—as Vatican II's *Lumen Gentium* teaches—are called to "consecrate the world to God" by living faithfully in families, workplaces, and civil society. To render to Caesar what is Caesar's is to give just service in the temporal order. But to render to God what is God's is to let that service be transfigured by charity and governed by truth.

In an age of political tribalism, when Caesar's image is stamped on every headline and ideology, the Church must form men and women who bear another image—Christ's. The world is watching not for slogans but for saints—those whose lives testify that Christ alone is Lord, and that no power on earth can rival the splendor of a soul totally given to God.

You bear God's image. You were purchased not with silver coins, but with the Blood of the Lamb. You belong not to Caesar, but to the Crucified and Risen Lord.

So give Caesar what is his—your taxes, your civic responsibilities. But give God what is His—your heart, your will, your entire life. For in the end, the image we bear at death will not be of any worldly empire, but of the Son of God who said, *"Follow me."*

May we render ourselves entirely to the Father, in union with Christ, through the Holy Spirit, and so become what we were created to be: the living icon of divine love in the world.

Thirtieth Sunday in Ordinary Time

Today we reach the very heart of the Gospel. In response to a question meant to test Him, Christ reveals not only the greatest commandment, but the true structure of Christian life: love of God and love of neighbor, not as separate paths, but as two dimensions of the one law of love.

In the Gospel, Jesus unites two commandments from the Torah—Deuteronomy 6:5 and Leviticus 19:18—and shows that the entire Law and the Prophets "hang" upon them. The Greek verb *krematai* (Mt 22:40) implies dependence and integration: all the precepts, moral and ritual, find their fulfillment and coherence in the double command of love.

For Saint Thomas Aquinas, love is not merely one virtue among many—it is the *form* of the virtues (*STh* II-II, q.23, a.8). Without charity, no other virtue can be true. It is charity that gives life to faith, purpose to justice, and direction to hope. Aquinas teaches that the love of God is the final end of the moral life, while the love of neighbor is the means through which we express that love concretely (*STh* II-II, q.25, a.1).

But this is not a merely ethical command. The true meaning of love is revealed only in Christ. In His incarnate life, especially in the Cross, we see love of the Father and love of humanity united without division or confusion. The Lord's perfect obedience to the Father *is* His perfect gift to us. Love, therefore, is theological before it is ethical. We do not generate it—it is given.

"You shall love the Lord your God with all your heart, soul, and mind." This is not an emotional command. It is a totalizing one.

Christ calls for an integrated, undivided love—affective (heart), vital (soul), and rational (mind). Nothing is to be held back.

But this love is not sentimental. Christian love is *not first our response*, but God's initiative. *"God has loved us first."* The theological virtue of charity is not something we manufacture. It is infused by the Holy Spirit. Thus, we are not only commanded to love; we are empowered to love through grace.

This is the love we return in worship, in fidelity to doctrine, and in trustful surrender—especially in suffering. The true love of God is a kenosis—a self-emptying that mirrors Christ's obedience to the Father: *"Love does not hold onto itself. It opens itself, loses itself, in God."*

The second commandment is like the first: *"You shall love your neighbor as yourself."* The "likeness" is not equality of importance but similarity of origin. Love of neighbor flows from love of God; it is its necessary expression. To love God is to love what God loves—especially the poor, the stranger, the vulnerable.

This is echoed in today's first reading from Exodus: *"You shall not wrong the alien... or the widow... or the orphan.* "These are not optional moral causes; they are the litmus test of covenant fidelity.

Christian love is never abstract. It has a face. It has a name. The Eucharist, which unites us to Christ, necessarily opens us to the other. Every act of charity is Eucharistic—because it is rooted in the same gift: Christ giving Himself *for us.*

The Church, then, is not first an institution of worship or even teaching, but a communion formed by love, from love, and for love. Love without truth becomes sentimentality, and truth without love becomes ideology. The Christian is called to hold both—to speak the truth in love and to live love in truth.

In a time when love is reduced to personal preference or tolerance, the Gospel calls us to a love that is absolute—because it is anchored in God Himself. This love is not always comfortable. It is cruciform. It requires discipline, sacrifice, and continual conversion. And yet, it is the only path to joy.

This theme becomes especially poignant as we approach the feasts of All Saints and All Souls, when the Church lifts our eyes to the final fruit of this twofold commandment. The saints—canonized or hidden—are those who have perfected the double love of God and neighbor, not by their own efforts, but by yielding to grace. They are the radiant proof that the Great Commandment is not an ideal; it is a destiny.

The saints make love visible in history because they allow divine charity to become their whole being. They are Eucharistic persons: given, broken, poured out. They wear the form of Christ crucified and glorified, which is the full expression of loving God *and* neighbor to the end.

And the faithful departed, remembered on All Souls' Day, are those being purified in love. Purgatory is not as a waiting room, but as a process of being conformed to Love—a painful joy, where every residue of self-enclosure is burned away by the fire of divine mercy. The souls in purgatory are on their way to that same fulfillment of the twofold commandment, longing for the face of the God they now love with increasing clarity.

To live now in this love—of God and neighbor—is to begin heaven on earth. To resist this love is to begin separation from the only reality that lasts.

The Lord today gives us the one measure by which our lives will be judged: Did you love God with everything? Did you love your neighbor as yourself? Not sentimentally. Not selectively. But wholly and sacrificially, in union with the Cross.

Let us take this Word to heart. Let us go to the altar where Love is made flesh, and ask to be drawn into that same offering. And let us live, even now, as citizens of the City of Love, together with the saints who intercede for us and the holy souls who long to see His face.

For this is the meaning of our lives: *to love and to become love*. And this is the promise of our destiny: *to see Love face to face*.

Thirty-First Sunday in Ordinary Time

As we move toward the end of the liturgical year, the Church gently but firmly turns our attention to the end—not as a cause for fear, but as an invitation to reflection. The Gospel today strikes a note of deep interior examination: "The greatest among you must be your servant. Whoever exalts himself will be humbled; but whoever humbles himself will be exalted" (Mt 23:11–12).

Last week, Christ gave us the double commandment of love—of God and of neighbor—as the essence of the law and the measure of judgment. Today, He warns us that the external appearance of religiosity can easily mask an inner emptiness, and that true greatness is measured not by titles, but by humility.

This is not merely a critique of the Pharisees of old. It is a prophetic warning to every believer, especially to those entrusted with teaching, preaching, and spiritual leadership. As the Church enters November—a month of remembrance, judgment, and hope—Christ reminds us that what truly matters is not what others see, but what God sees. The final judgment will not weigh appearances but hearts; it will reveal the truth of our loves.

"They preach but do not practice." Jesus' critique is not aimed at doctrine but at disconnection—between the Word of God and the interior life. The Pharisees "sit on Moses' seat," but they have not allowed that Word to transform them. Their devotion has become performance; their service, self-display.

Saint Thomas Aquinas teaches that hypocrisy is not merely moral inconsistency, but the act of "appearing to be virtuous when one is not" (*STh* II–II, q.111, a.1). It is a sin against truth—against the integrity of one's relationship with God. The hypocrite may still perform good works, but they are directed toward self rather than toward God. The danger is subtle but real: we can do the right things for the wrong reasons.

God desires truth in the inward being (Ps 51:6). He desires the unity of heart and deed, of faith and charity. External observance without interior conversion cannot endure. What the Lord seeks is not theatrical holiness but sincerity of heart.

In contrast to the Pharisees, Jesus points to the humble servant: "Whoever humbles himself will be exalted." This reversal is not accidental—it is the very rhythm of the Gospel. Christ's self-emptying— His *kenosis*—is not a tragic exception, but the revelation of divine love itself. True glory is found not in thrones, but on the Cross. To prepare for heaven, we must learn the movement of descent—the willingness to take the lowest place before God and neighbor.

This truth is mirrored in the saints we have just celebrated and the faithful departed we now remember. The saints were not those who exalted themselves, but those who allowed God to shape them in the quiet fidelity of daily life—in their homes, in their work, in the hidden service of love. Their greatness was not in visibility, but in availability to grace.

The journey toward holiness is, in the end, a journey downward—a stripping away of masks, roles, and pretenses until the soul stands as it is before God. At the hour of death, nothing remains but love. Our prayer today, then, becomes a preparation for that final encounter, where we no longer speak many words, but simply become what we have prayed.

Saint Thomas reminds us that humility is the foundation of the spiritual life because it orders the soul rightly before God (*STh* II–II, q.161, a.5). In humility, we see ourselves as we truly are: utterly dependent on grace, yet infinitely loved. This is not humiliation—it is truth, and truth is the beginning of freedom.

The path forward, then, is the life of prayer—not mechanical recitation, but contemplative openness before God. In prayer, we surrender the masks we wear. We learn to acknowledge our poverty and allow the Holy Spirit to reorder our affections and desires. Prayer becomes the school of humility, the place where the Word pierces through our self-deception and re-creates us in honesty.

When we pray with the Scriptures, when we reflect each evening on how we have loved or failed to love, when we sit silently before the Eucharist and allow ourselves to be seen—these are not small acts. They are the slow work of sanctification. In such prayer, we are drawn out of self and into communion.

The titles of "rabbi," "father," and "master" do not scandalize Christ when they are used in service of truth and love. What offends Him is when external honor replaces interior holiness. And so He calls us back to simplicity: "You have one Father—the one in heaven. You have one Teacher—the Christ."

Let us, then, enter the inner room of the heart and live before the face of the Father. Let us call no one Master but Christ, not merely with our lips but with our lives.

For the end will come, and when it does, we will not be asked what titles we had or how many followed us, but whether we loved in secret, prayed with sincerity, and humbled ourselves before the One who alone is holy.

Thirty-Second Sunday in Ordinary Time

We have entered the final stretch of the liturgical year, and the Church, like a wise mother, turns our eyes toward the end—not as catastrophe, but as consummation. The Gospel parable of the ten virgins is a summons to vigilance, readiness, and interior depth. It is not enough to carry a lamp. One must also have oil.

This is not a lesson in preparedness techniques. It is a parable about the interior life, the necessity of grace, and the reality that not all who seem ready truly are. The Church is not warning us simply of death, but of the possibility of missing the Bridegroom even while standing near the door.

The parable is simple in structure. Ten virgins await the bridegroom. All have lamps, all grow drowsy, all fall asleep. But when the call goes out at midnight, only five have oil. The others beg, scramble, and finally return too late. *"Amen, I say to you, I do not know you."*

What distinguishes the wise from the foolish? Not proximity. Not desire. Not even belief. All were waiting. The difference lies in what was hidden: the inner reserve of oil—symbol of the interior life, of sanctifying grace, of habitual friendship with the Bridegroom.

Saint Thomas Aquinas teaches that the oil signifies charity, the infused virtue by which the soul lives in union with God (*STh* II-II, q.24, a.3). Lamps without oil are like faith without love—visible, even functional, but ultimately dead (*cf.* James 2:17). The foolish virgins presume they can borrow what cannot be transferred: the personal substance of a life lived in grace.

The great spiritual crisis of our time is not disbelief, but distraction—the illusion that the Bridegroom can be met without interior preparation. We must not only believe in His coming—we must long for it.

The first reading from the Book of Wisdom speaks of this inner readiness: *"Wisdom is radiant and unfading... she hastens to make herself known to those who desire her"* (Wis 6:12–13). Wisdom, in the biblical sense, is not cleverness—it is the virtue of living in harmony with God's will. The wise soul lives in attentive prayer, expectant trust, and disciplined love.

To live wisely is to live informed by the Cross, to see reality through the eyes of the Bridegroom who comes not in spectacle, but in silence. The wise virgins are those who have kept vigil not only with their minds, but with their hearts—who have let the Paschal form of Christ shape their whole being.

The "oil" cannot be bought in a moment because it is the slow product of daily surrender—of silent prayer, of repeated repentance, of small acts of love hidden from the world. This oil accumulates drop by drop, often unnoticed, but it burns brightly when all else fails.

The Bridegroom arrives at midnight—the hour of darkness, the hour of decision, the hour of divine reversal. Midnight is the symbol of death, of crisis, of the final judgment. It is also the moment of joyful surprise: *"Blessed are those servants whom the master finds awake when he comes."* (Lk 12:37)

This is why prayer is not merely a duty—it is existential readiness. The soul that prays—daily, silently, honestly—is like a lamp constantly trimmed. It may appear unimpressive. But at midnight, it shines.

Let us then consider our prayer lives in light of the end. Is prayer a task to accomplish, or a flame to nurture? Do we pray from the surface, or from the depths? Have we accumulated oil in our hearts— or are we assuming that, somehow, grace can be borrowed at the last?

The Church is to form saints, not functionaries." And saints are those who have kept vigil through the long night—not perfectly, but faithfully, often with nothing more than a flickering flame, trusting that the Bridegroom sees and knows.

As we continue the Church's November pilgrimage—remembering the saints and praying for the dead—let us recommit ourselves to interior watchfulness. Here are three simple practices for storing oil: first, praying a morning offering, beginning each day consciously giving your heart, work, and suffering to God. This orientates the entire day toward the Bridegroom; second, silent prayer – Even ten minutes a day in silence before the Lord, especially in Eucharistic Adoration, deepens the inner reservoir of grace; third and finally, making intercession for the dying – adopting the practice of praying for those who will die that day. It connects your vigil to the universal Church and prepares your own heart for that hour.

These practices are not about performance. They are about presence. They make space for oil to accumulate—not from you, but from the Holy Spirit.

"And the door was shut." (Mt 25:10) These are among the most chilling words in the Gospel. Not because God is cruel, but because grace, once refused, cannot be pretended. The Bridegroom desires our presence—but He will not be manipulated by our delays.

Let us live now in readiness—not in fear, but in love. For the Bridegroom is near. And when He comes—perhaps at midnight, perhaps today—may we hear Him say not *"I do not know you,"* but rather: *"Come, share your Master's joy."*

Thirty-Third Sunday in Ordinary Time

As we near the end of the liturgical year, the Church's tone becomes more urgent, more eschatological. The readings lead us to reflect on what endures and what perishes, on what we have done with the grace entrusted to us. Last Sunday, we heard of the wise and foolish virgins—those who kept watch and those who failed to prepare. Next Sunday, on the Solemnity of Christ the King, we will stand before the final judgment. But today, in this "penultimate" parable, the Lord teaches us about stewardship, courage, and the investment of grace.

We are not asked merely to wait for the Bridegroom—we are asked to labor while He delays. The Gospel of the talents reminds us that Christian life is not passive waiting for rescue, but active fidelity to mission. Each of us has been entrusted with gifts that belong not to us, but to God.

It is tempting to read this parable as a lesson in productivity or personal development. But the "talents" here are not primarily natural abilities or social advantages. They symbolize the graces of the Kingdom—divine gifts entrusted for the good of others and the glory of God. Saint Thomas Aquinas teaches that grace builds upon nature (*STh* I, q.1, a.8) but always transcends it. Grace perfects, heals, and elevates what is human, calling it into divine purpose. The talents, then, represent everything we receive from God: our faith, our vocation, our charisms, our opportunities to love. These are not possessions to guard; they are graces to steward.

To bury a talent is not simply laziness—it is a refusal to trust the Master. The fearful servant accuses God of being harsh: "I knew you were a demanding man..." (Mt 25:24). But the real root of his failure is not sloth—it is fear rooted in a distorted image of God. The servant hides his gift because he does not believe in the generosity of the Giver.

Our second reading tells us that "the day of the Lord will come like a thief in the night" (1 Thess 5:2). These words are not meant to frighten, but to awaken us. God delays not to frustrate us, but to give us time—time for fidelity, creativity, and love. Just as the virgins were called to keep watch, so now the servants are called to act.

Our Lord does not ask us to return His gifts untouched. He wants to see them multiplied in charity—through works of mercy, through patient endurance, through fidelity in small things, through courage in witness. The one who truly knows God does not hide the light of grace but risks sharing it.

Saint Thomas teaches that charity gives form and purpose to all the virtues (*STh* II–II, q.23, a.8). Without charity, even our greatest efforts are sterile; but with it, every small act becomes eternal. True fruitfulness is not measured in quantity but in faithfulness. The smallest investment of love, when offered with humility, grows into something divine.

The servant who buried his talent did not lose it by accident—he forfeited it by fear. He imagined God as a tyrant, not a Father. And so he lived closed in on himself, unwilling to risk love. The tragedy of his life is not his failure, but his mistrust. The judgment he receives—being cast into darkness—is not simply punishment but the revelation of what he has chosen: a life turned inward, without light, without joy.

The faithful servants, by contrast, saw the Master as good and worthy of their effort. They risked their time, their energy, and their hearts because they trusted His character. They acted not to impress Him, but to participate in His joy. "Well done, good and faithful servant," the Master says, "enter into the joy of your Lord." (Mt 25:23).

This is the heart of all Christian stewardship. It is not fear of condemnation, but love that longs to give something back—not to earn God's approval, but to express gratitude for what He has already given. Every grace we receive is an invitation to communion. To invest our talents is to live generously—to let our lives become fruitful through love.

The true investment of divine gifts happens quietly, in prayer and in charity. The heart of the disciple is a place of divine exchange, where the goods of God are multiplied by surrender. To invest the talent is not to achieve worldly success, but to offer what we have received back to the Giver, enlarged through love.

Each day, the Lord entrusts us anew with His grace—in the sacraments, in our prayer, in our relationships, and in the hidden tasks of life. Every encounter becomes an opportunity to grow in charity, the greatest of all treasures. We do not measure the increase of grace as we would earthly profit; we measure it by the expansion of the heart.

As we prepare for the Solemnity of Christ the King and the close of the liturgical year, this parable leaves us with a question that is both searching and consoling: What have we done with the grace entrusted to us? Have we risked love? Have we multiplied mercy? Have we entered into the work of the Kingdom—or have we buried our gifts out of fear?

Now is the time to act—not someday, not when life is calmer or conditions are perfect—but now. For the Master will return. And His judgment will not be a surprise; it will be the unveiling of who we have become by grace. If we have spent ourselves in love, if we have trusted the Master's goodness and shared His gifts with others, then we will hear the words every heart longs for:

"Well done, good and faithful servant… enter into my joy."

Solemnity of Our Lord Jesus Christ, King of the Universe

Today the Church, in her wisdom and joy, crowns the liturgical year with the Solemnity of Christ the King—a feast not born in ancient times, but in the modern world's hour of crisis. Pope Pius XI instituted this feast in 1925 amid the ashes of World War I, the rise of secularism, nationalism, and totalitarianism, to boldly proclaim a truth the world desperately needed then and still needs now: Jesus Christ is Lord—of history, of nations, of every human heart.

This is not the kingship of Caesar or Pharaoh. This is the kingship of the Crucified and Risen One—a kingship of truth, love, and mercy. And in today's Gospel, we meet Him enthroned—not on a battlefield, but in judgment over the nations, separating sheep from goats not by race, wealth, or power, but by charity: *"Whatever you did for one of the least of these, you did it for me."*

In Matthew 25, we hear the great scene of the Final Judgment, which the Fathers of the Church always interpreted as a revelation of the deepest truth of Christian life. Saint John Chrysostom preached that this Gospel teaches not only about judgment, but about the intimacy between Christ and the poor:

"If you wish to honor the body of Christ, do not despise Him when He is naked. Do not honor Him in the church with silk vestments while you leave Him cold outside and unclothed." (*Homily on Matthew 50*)

This is the paradox of the King: He is hidden in the hungry and the thirsty, the imprisoned and the stranger. To love the least is to love the King.

In the first reading from Ezekiel 34, God declares that He Himself will shepherd His people. The context is important: Israel's leaders—their "shepherds"—had failed. So God promises: *"I myself will look after my sheep."*

Here, as the Fathers saw, is a foreshadowing of the Incarnation. God does not send another prophet—He comes in person. In Jesus, the Shepherd King walks among His sheep, seeks out the lost, binds up the wounded, and lays down His life.

This is kingship not as domination, but as self-giving. The throne is the Cross. The crown is thorns. And His power is not coercion, but kenosis—self-emptying.

Saint Paul, in the second reading, gives us a cosmic vision: *Christ must reign until He has put all His enemies under His feet... and then the Son will hand over the kingdom to the Father.* (1 Cor 15:24)

This is not the image of an isolated monarch. It is Trinitarian. Christ's kingship is always filial: He reigns as Son, and He hands all back to the Father in love.

This is not just Christ's destiny—it is our calling. We, too, must reign by loving, by becoming Eucharistic, by allowing our lives to be handed over in service, just as Christ does.

The kingship of Christ is not merely a future reality. It is the task of the Church today to proclaim and embody this reign in history. Pope Pius XI, in his encyclical *Quas Primas*, warned that when societies refuse to recognize Christ's authority, they do not become neutral—they become idolatrous, and power, pleasure, and politics become false gods.

We must let His reign be seen in our works of mercy, our reverence for the Eucharist, our fidelity to truth, our protection of the vulnerable, and our joyful hope in the life to come.

Christ the King is not far. He is already among us—in the Eucharist, in the poor, in His Word, in the suffering, and in our neighbor. And He will come again in glory. When He does, He will ask not how much we achieved or accumulated, but how much we loved.

Saint Augustine once said: *"Let us not resist His first coming, so that we may not dread His second."*

Let us then surrender now to His reign. Let us build the Kingdom here—by mercy, by justice, by humility—so that on the Last Day, we may hear those blessed words: *"Come, you who are blessed by my Father. Inherit the kingdom prepared for you from the foundation of the world."*

www.ingramcontent.com/pod-product-compliance
Lightning Source LLC
Chambersburg PA
CBHW070018100426
42740CB00013B/2550